It Happened to Me

Series Editor: Arlene Hirschfelder

Books in the It Happened to Me series are designed for inquisitive teens digging for answers about certain illnesses, social issues, or lifestyle interests. Whether you are deep into your teen years or just entering them, these books are gold mines of up-to-date information, riveting teen views, and great visuals to help you figure out stuff. Besides special boxes highlighting singular facts, each book is enhanced with the latest reading lists, websites, and an index. Perfect for browsing, these books contain loads of expert information by acclaimed writers to help parents, guardians, and librarians understand teen illness, tough situations, and lifestyle choices.

1. *Epilepsy: The Ultimate Teen Guide*, by Kathlyn Gay and Sean McGarrahan, 2002.
2. *Stress Relief: The Ultimate Teen Guide*, by Mark Powell, 2002.
3. *Learning Disabilities: The Ultimate Teen Guide*, by Penny Hutchins Paquette and Cheryl Gerson Tuttle, 2003.
4. *Making Sexual Decisions: The Ultimate Teen Guide*, by L. Kris Gowen, 2003.
5. *Asthma: The Ultimate Teen Guide*, by Penny Hutchins Paquette, 2003.
6. *Cultural Diversity—Conflicts and Challenges: The Ultimate Teen Guide*, by Kathlyn Gay, 2003.
7. *Diabetes: The Ultimate Teen Guide*, by Katherine J. Moran, 2004.
8. *When Will I Stop Hurting? Teens, Loss, and Grief: The Ultimate Teen Guide to Dealing with Grief*, by Ed Myers, 2004.
9. *Volunteering: The Ultimate Teen Guide*, by Kathlyn Gay, 2004.
10. *Organ Transplants—A Survival Guide for the Entire Family: The Ultimate Teen Guide*, by Tina P. Schwartz, 2005.

The Military and Teens

The Ultimate Teen Guide

KATHLYN GAY

It Happened to Me, No. 21

The Scarecrow Press, Inc.
Lanham, Maryland • Toronto • Plymouth, UK
2008

SCARECROW PRESS, INC.

Published in the United States of America
by Scarecrow Press, Inc.
A wholly owned subsidary of
The Rowman & Littlefield Publishing Group, Inc.
4501 Forbes Boulevard, Suite 200, Lanham, Maryland 20706
www.scarecrowpress.com

Estover Road
Plymouth PL6 7PY
United Kingdom

British Library Cataloguing in Publication Information Available

Library of Congress Cataloging-in-Publication Data

Gay, Kathlyn.
  The military and teens : the ultimate teen guide / Kathlyn Gay.
    p. cm. — (It happened to me ; no. 21)
  Includes bibliographical references and index.
  ISBN-13: 978-0-8108-5801-5 (hbk. : alk. paper)
  ISBN-10: 0-8108-5801-0 (hbk. : alk. paper)
  1. United States—Armed Forces—Vocational guidance. 2. United States—Armed Forces—Recruiting,
enlistment, etc. 3. Military service, Voluntary—United States. 4. Conscientious objectors—United States.
I. Title.
  UB323.G38 2008
  355.0023'73—dc22   2007050480

⊗™ The paper used in this publication meets the minimum requirements of
American National Standard for Information Sciences—Permanence of Paper
for Printed Library Materials, ANSI/NISO Z39.48-1992.
Manufactured in the United States of America.

Contents

1

Who Defends the Nation?

Evan Hoke is just one of the many young people planning to defend the nation. Another is Matthew Detrick, of Great Falls, Montana. When he was a high school senior in 2006, he explained that he intended to enlist in the military to "protect America and the people in it."[2] Travon A. Turner, a teen in Los Angeles, said he never wanted to serve in the armed forces but had long dreamed of being an engineer for the Department of Defense (DoD). "I want to invent the types of weapons that will protect the United States and other countries without killing people," he said.[3] Teenager Colin Smith of Virginia joined the U.S. Marines because he says, "I'd like to protect my country. . . . I have a lot of faith in my country."[4]

   Although these comments represent the opinions of some Americans who are or could be defending the nation in war, many others express antiwar sentiments and have no intention of serving in the volunteer military. Conflicting opinions about military service are nothing new. The pros and cons of taking up arms have been articulated by Americans since colonial times.

"I've decided to join the U.S. Air Force. . . . I've always believed that people should do their part to help make a better future and help defend what we have."

—teenager Evan Hoke of Pennsylvania[1]

REVOLUTIONARY DEFENDERS AND OPPONENTS

As is well known, American colonists were divided in their views about waging war to gain freedom from British rule. Yet, an estimated 290,000 colonists fought in the war for independence. Many who went into battle were teenagers like Joseph Plumb Martin, who at first wanted nothing to do with war. But as the British became increasingly oppressive, colonial leaders called for farmers and townspeople, who became known as patriots or rebels, to join their local militias and be prepared to defend their communities. Martin enlisted at the age of fifteen in a private Connecticut regiment for six months; then in 1777, at sixteen years old, he joined the Continental army commanded by General George Washington and served for six years.[5]

Some colonial youth became involved in the military when they were preteens, serving in militia drum-and-fife corps.

A REVOLUTIONARY "DRAFT DODGER"

Samuel Shelby, who was born in 1760, made no secret of the fact that he was a draft dodger during the Revolutionary War. He did enter the service at the age of twenty but not before he attempted to pass as an adolescent (he looked much younger than his actual age) to avoid the military. According to Shelby's own account published in a collection of military records, he:

> enlisted under the following circumstances. There were two American officers came to my father's at Canoe Brook [New Jersey] and desired a conveyance to Green Brook. My father sent me with them. This was in the month of March. I traveled in a sleigh across the fields and over the fences. . . . When we arrived at Green Brook, I was asked concerning my age. I told them I was twelve. They let me pass and I returned home. When I reached home . . . an orderly sergeant in the army came and inquired my age. I told him the same thing. He then went to an old aunt of mine who was ignorant of his purpose, and from her he learned the truth. He then said to me, "My fine fellow . . . Do you not know that there is a heavy fine if you do not join the army when you get to your age?" I told him I did not. He then carried me off to Green Brook on a sleigh. When there [they] told me I had better enlist for nine months and then they would give me clear, and I accordingly did so.[6]

In 2006, soldiers demonstrate the role of skirmishers at a celebration commemorating the 225th anniversary of the American victory at Yorktown, Virginia, during the Revolutionary War. Photo by Spc. Van Der Weide, courtesy U.S. Army.

John Greenwood was an example. An excellent fifer at ten years old, he joined the Massachusetts militia under Captain Martin Gay, and by the time he turned fifteen, the Revolutionary War was underway, and he was in the midst of it, fighting for independence.[7]

The long war officially ended when the United States and Great Britain signed the Treaty of Paris in September 1783. General George Washington became the first president of the new nation, and six years later, the United States established a national army. In a letter to the First Congress, Washington declared that the "honor, safety and well-being of our Country" depended on establishing a national armed force.[8] On September 29, 1789, the U.S. Congress passed "an act to recognize and adapt to the Constitution of the United States, the establishment of the troops raised under the resolves of the United States in Congress assembled."[9] The act officially created the U.S. military.

CITIZEN MILITIAS

Long before the Revolutionary War, each colony had its own militia, citizen soldiers who provided a colony's defense. Colonial laws required all able-bodied white men to join the militia, although the laws were not strictly enforced in some colonies. Usually men volunteered for the militia, but some paid a fine rather than serve.

Colonial militias were organized in pyramid fashion, with companies, regiments, and brigades commanded by a civil authority. A local authority or leader could call up the militia, and fighting in the American Revolution began with mobilization of local units who ranged in age from sixteen to sixty. They trained on specific days of the week, bringing their own rifles or muskets and ammunition.

When the Continental Congress authorized George Washington to establish a Continental army, Washington had to discipline some militia to stay with their units rather than return home when there was a lull in the shooting. Eventually, of course, the Continental army won the war, while local militia successfully defended the home front.

The U.S. Constitution adopted in 1787 declares that the president is the "Commander in Chief of the Army and Navy of the United States, and of the Militia of the several States when called into the actual Service of the United States." The U.S. Congress, however, has the power to call "forth the Militia to execute the Laws of the Union, suppress Insurrections and repel Invasions; To provide for organizing, arming, and disciplining the Militia, and governing such part of them as may be employed in the service of the United States."

CREATING ARMED FORCES

In Washington's time, the U.S. Army consisted of only one thousand men, and after the Revolution, Congress discharged the army except for about one hundred soldiers and officers who guarded military supplies at Fort Pitt and West Point. According to David and Mady Segal writing for the *Population Bulletin*, "This congressional action set a precedent for a military force . . . that was to be mobilized during wartime through calling up the militia, recruiting volunteers, and occasional conscription, and was to be demobilized during peacetime."[10]

For example, a fighting force for the War of 1812 was recruited from state militias after war was declared. Troops served in the regular army, which consisted of about ten thousand men at the time, although Congress mandated several increases in the army's strength during the two years of the war.[11]

At the beginning of the U.S. Civil War, tens of thousands of militiamen volunteered to serve on both the Union and Confederate sides. But that initial support for war soon declined, and some states began compulsory service. Manpower needs were not met, however, and both the North and South enacted draft laws. The U.S. Congress passed the Enrollment Act of 1863, requiring all able-bodied men between the ages of twenty and forty-five to serve in the military. But a man could pay a substitute to take his place, allowing a rich person to stay home while a poor man had to fight. After the war, the military population declined, and the force that remained fought primarily on the Western frontier against Native Americans who were defending their homelands and resisting the expansion of white culture.

In 1898, the Spanish-American War erupted. The United States fought Spain's brutal suppression of its colonists in Cuba, a war that the government justified on the grounds that Spain's actions were a threat to U.S. security. The bulk of the U.S. men who served were inducted into the volunteer state militias. As had been true since the Revolution, the U.S. War Department relied on its citizen forces to fight in the trenches and on the ships. State militia units included Theodore Roosevelt's Rough Riders (first U.S. volunteer cavalry), who became legendary due to Roosevelt's published accounts of their exploits. But the navy conducted most of the major battles and achieved "unparalleled victories" for the United States, as the secretary of the navy reported.[12]

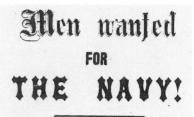

Men wanted

FOR

THE NAVY!

All able bodied men and boys

Will be enlisted into the NAVAL SERVICE upon application at the Naval Rendezvous.

Come forward and serve your Country

WITHOUT CONSCRIPTION!

Roanoke Island, Dec. 8th, 1863.

Photo # 45-X-11   Navy Recruiting Poster, 1863

This Civil War recruitment poster was published on behalf of the Naval Rendezvous, Roanoke Island, North Carolina, in December 1863. Photo from the Naval Records Collection in the U.S. National Archives.

Even when the United States entered World War I, the military depended on the volunteer militia who joined draftees inducted under the Selective Service Act of 1917. World War II changed the "surge and decline" pattern of the armed forces. As the Segals explain:

> About 16 million people were brought into the armed forces in the 1940s, including more than 200,000 women. The men were largely conscripts (10.1 million); women were not subject to the draft, and all women in uniform were volunteers. The World War II armed forces represented about 12 percent of the population and included about 56 percent of the men eligible for military service on the basis of age, health, and mental aptitude.[13]

Through the Korean and Vietnam conflicts, the draft continued, but in 1973, as the United States began to reduce troops in Vietnam, service in the U.S. armed forces became voluntary. In 1975, after the end of the Vietnam War, mandatory registration for the draft ended, but in 1980, during the administration of President Jimmy Carter, the Soviets invaded Afghanistan, and U.S. registration for a possible draft was resumed. Today, young men are required to register with the Selective Service System in the event that conscription should be necessary.

Clearly, the number of recruits in the armed forces has varied greatly throughout U.S. history. At the end of April 2007, more than 1.3 million active-duty personnel were serving in the five branches of the U.S. armed forces—Army, Navy, Marine Corps, Air Force, and Coast Guard. The largest branch is the U.S. Army, with 506,546 active-duty soldiers in April 2007, according to the DoD.[14]

NATURALIZED MILITARY MEMBERS

In July 2002, President George W. Bush signed Executive Order 13269, which allows foreign-born, legally permanent residents actively serving in the U.S. military and honorably discharged legally permanent residents who were on active duty on or after September 11, 2001, to be immediately eligible to apply for naturalization. The president can authorize accelerated applications during periods in which the United States is engaged in armed conflict with a hostile foreign force. Previously, noncitizens in the armed forces had to serve three years before they could apply for citizenship.

Army Specialist Maria Juarez at Fort Sam Houston in Texas is one soldier who was able to apply for citizenship. The September 11, 2001, attack on the United States prompted Juarez, a native of Zacatecas, Mexico, to join the military because she believed war was imminent and she

DID YOU KNOW?

Since the 1960s, the U.S. Navy has used dolphins and sea lions to patrol naval bases in coastal states. The mammals have sonar abilities and can dive deep in the ocean. They are trained to detect mines and even enemy divers. In 2003, dolphins were deployed to a port at Umm Qasr, Iraq, to detect underwater mines.

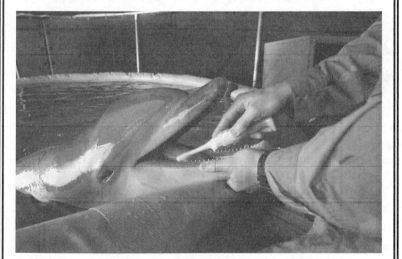

A mammal handler cares for a bottle-nosed dolphin by brushing its teeth in the well deck aboard USS *Gunston Hall*. Photo by Brien Aho, courtesy U.S. Navy.

FOUR-LEGGED SOLDIERS

Dogs have been used in war since ancient times, usually to warn that enemies were approaching or to attack in battle. The First American Canine Corp appeared during the 1800s in wars with the Seminoles and also in the Civil War, when dogs were used as messengers and guards. They also were scouts in the Spanish-American War. But the value of military dogs was not recognized widely until World War II.

After the Japanese attack on the U.S. naval base at Pearl Harbor, the Military Working Dog (MWD) Program was established. The American Kennel Club and a group known as Dogs for Defense encouraged dog owners to donate suitable animals to the U.S. Army Quartermaster Corps. The Quartermasters were in charge of the Canine Corps, or K-9 Corps, a popular term for the military dogs as well as those used for security in private life. According to the Military Working Dog Foundation, "At first more than thirty breeds were accepted. Later the list was narrowed down to German Shepherds, Belgian Sheep Dogs, Doberman Pinschers, Farm Collies and Giant Schnauzers."[15]

MWDs have been an important part of the U.S. armed forces since World War II. Dogs are trained to carry messages under fire, act as scout dogs to sense enemy presence at a greater distance than is possible for humans to detect, find booby traps and mines, discover casualties, and save lives.

Some dogs have been so outstanding that they have been honored. For example, Staff Sgt. Wendy, an explosive detection dog, was awarded an Army Commendation Medal for her work in Afghanistan where she helped protect numerous soldiers. She

died in 2006 and received full military burial. However, military dogs are not eligible for high honors, such as a Bronze Star or Purple Heart, because they are nonhumans. Nevertheless, some unit commanders have pinned unofficial medals on their MWDs. The U.S. War Dogs Association is one group petitioning for a U.S. K-9 Military Service Medal as a way to commend the four-legged soldiers for their combat contributions.

Air Force Staff Sgt. Ian Spivey and his military working dog, Rex, help search vehicles at a traffic control point in Baghdad, Iraq, January 2007. Photo by Sgt. Richard Kolberg, courtesy U.S. Army.

One MWD widely recognized was Chips, who served in North Africa, Sicily, Italy, France, and Germany during World War II. Disney produced a TV movie titled *Chips the War Dog*, which was released in 1993.[16] Current endeavors for MWD recognition include a campaign to establish a national monument in honor of military working dog teams.

"wanted to give something back. . . . I wanted to help this country that had given me and my family opportunity,"[17] she told a reporter. In 2002, while she was in her early twenties, Juarez enlisted in the armed forces. She was able to do so after she got her green card. In order to enlist, noncitizen recruits must hold a green card or have legal permanent residence status as confirmed by the Citizenship and Immigration Services, pass a test for English-language skills, and clear criminal background checks. Juarez served for a year in Iraq, and at the age of twenty-five in 2006, she was ready to apply for naturalization. She noted, "I feel like an American, and now I want to be a citizen, to have my complete rights, to vote, and be part of the system."[18]

Expedited applications are finalized at U.S. military bases and medical centers; on U.S. ships; and overseas at U.S. embassies, consulates, and selected military installations. Ceremonies for soldiers, airmen, sailors, and marines have been held in Afghanistan, Djibouti, Germany, Greece, Iceland, Iraq, Italy, Japan, Kenya, Kuwait, South Korea, Spain, the United Kingdom, and in the Pacific aboard the USS *Kitty Hawk*. On Veterans' Day, November 11, 2006, for example, military naturalization services were held in Iraq and Afghanistan, where a total of 136 service members became citizens. On November 12, another forty-four service members in Iraq were naturalized, and on November 14, 2006, at the U.S. consulate, Frankfurt, Germany, twenty-nine service members received their citizenship. Each year, nearly seven thousand members of the armed forces have been naturalized through the expedited process.[19]

NOTES

1. "In Their Own Words: Future Plans," *eJournal USA* (electronic journal of the U.S. State Department), July 2005, usinfo.state.gov/journals/itsv/0705/ijse/future.htm (accessed June 24, 2007).

2. "State's Youth Open to Military," *National Guard Youth Challenge Program*, originally published in the *Great Falls Tribune*,

March 26, 2006, www.ngycp.org/vBulletin/showthread.php?t=5110 (accessed June 24, 2007).

3. Rudi Williams, "Teen Learns He Can Serve without Joining Military," *Kansas City infoZine*, October 7, 2005, www.infozine .com/news/stories/op/storiesView/sid/10710 (accessed June 24, 2007).

4. "In Their Own Words."

5. See Joseph Plumb Martin, *Private Yankee Doodle: Being a Narrative of Some of the Adventures, Dangers, and Sufferings of a Revolutionary Soldier*, ed. George E. Scheer (Boston: Little, Brown, 1962).

6. John C. Dann, ed., *The Revolution Remembered: Eyewitness Accounts of the War for Independence* (Chicago: University of Chicago Press, 1980), p. 128.

7. See John Greenwood, *A Young Patriot in the American Revolution 1775–1783: A Record of Events Written during the Year 1809 at Such Leisure Moments as the Arduous Duties of a Professional Life Permitted* (Tyrone, PA: Westvaco, 1981).

8. "An Act for the Establishment of Troops," *Today in History*, Library of Congress, n.d., memory.loc.gov/ammem/today/sep29.html (accessed June 23, 2007).

9. "Act for the Establishment of Troops."

10. David R. Segal and Mady Wechsler Segal, "America's Military Population," *Population Bulletin 59*, no. 4 (Washington, DC: Population Reference Bureau, 2004), p. 4.

11. "War of 1812 Discharge Certificates," U.S. National Archives and Records Administration, updated February 22, 2005, www.archives.gov/genealogy/military/1812/discharge-certificates.html?template=print#4 (accessed June 24, 2007).

12. John D. Long, "Annual Report of the Secretary of the Navy," in *Annual Reports of the Navy Department for the Year 1898* (Washington, DC: Government Printing Office, 1898), www.history.navy.mil/wars/spanam/sn98-1.htm (accessed June 23, 2007).

13. Segal and Segal, "America's Military Population," p. 4.

14. *Department of Defense Active Duty Military by Rank and Grade*, April 30, 2007, siadapp.dmdc.osd.mil/personnel/MILITARY/rg0704.pdf (accessed June 15, 2007).

15. "Military Working Dog History," *Military Working Dog Foundation*, n.d., www.militaryworkingdog.com/history (accessed June 23, 2007).

16. See Lisa Hoffman, "Giving War Dogs the Recognition They Deserve," *Capitol Hill Blue*, August 2, 2006, www.capitolhillblue .com/news2/2006/08/giving_war_dogs_the_recognition.html (accessed June 23, 2007).

17. Quoted in David McLemore, "Serving a Nation Not Yet Their Own," *Dallas Morning News*, November 28, 2006, www.dallasnews.com/sharedcontent/dws/news/texassouthwest/ stories/DN-immigmilitary_28tex.ART.North.Edition1.3e0efa3.html# (accessed June 16, 2007).

18. Quoted in McLemore, "Serving a Nation Not Yet Their Own."

19. "DHS/DoD Commemorates Veterans' Day by Welcoming America's Newest Citizens: Overseas Ceremonies Held in Afghanistan, Germany, and Iraq," Press Release, U.S. Department of Homeland Security, U.S. Citizenship and Immigration Services, November 17, 2006, www.uscis.gov/files/pressrelease/Iraqnatz_ 16no06.pdf (accessed June 23, 2007).

Who's Patriotic? What's Patriotism?

No doubt about it, "teens are patriotic," according to the Harrison Group, which surveyed teenagers in late 2006 to learn about trends and what teens want. The report states, "Fully 87 percent of teens said they are proud to be American."[2] But what does patriotism mean? Bonnie, whose words appear in the opening quote, also writes: "Love of country is not a single, superficial act but an all-encompassing feeling, and that love is demonstrated in the willingness to sacrifice oneself for certain ideals."[3] Nineteen-year-old Army Spc. Bruce Bryant expresses his patriotism not only as a member of the military but also as one of the sentinels who guards the tomb of the unknown soldier in Washington, DC. He says, "It makes you feel really good, really humble."[4]

Teenagers, as well as adults, show their patriotism in a variety of ways, often with items such as:

- A bracelet with an American flag charm;
- Patriotic shoes with red, white, and blue designs;
- American flag face plates for cell phones;
- Car flags;
- "Support Our Troops" car magnets;
- American flag pins;
- Red, white, and blue bead bracelets;
- USA necklaces; and
- Hats, shirts, and jackets with flag motifs.

"Patriotism is not just raising an American flag on your porch or buying a bumper sticker, it is a conscious state of being."

—Bonnie K., writing for *Teen Ink*, a monthly magazine and website[1]

WHAT'S A PATRIOT?—TWO VIEWS

"A patriot is a person who loves his or her country."[5] These words were the opening remarks of Mayor Ross C. "Rocky" Anderson of Salt Lake City, Utah. An opponent of the Iraq war, Anderson addressed a gathering of several thousand antiwar people in August 2006 and forcefully declared:

> Let no one deny we are patriots. We support our nation's troops. We are grateful to our veterans who have sacrificed so much for our freedoms. We love our country, we hold dear the values upon which our nation was founded. . . . Blind faith in bad leaders is not patriotism. A patriot does not tell people who are intensely concerned about their country to just sit down and be quiet; to refrain from speaking out in the name of politeness or for the sake of being a good host; to show slavish, blind obedience. . . . That is not a patriot. Rather, that person is a sycophant.[6]

Mayor Anderson ended his speech with an injunction from Dr. Martin Luther King Jr.: "Our lives begin to end the day we become silent about things that matter."[7]

Another view was expressed by Vice President Dick Cheney in 2006. He addressed families of the Indiana Army and Air National Guard at Camp Atterbury, Indiana, and presented his view about the Iraq War: "We are doing honorable work in a messy and a dangerous world. By defending ourselves, and by standing with our friends abroad, we're meeting our responsibilities as freedom's home and defender, and we are securing the peace that freedom brings."[8]

PATRIOTIC DUTY AND PATRIOTIC DISSENT

Every American war has produced propaganda that urges people to rally around the flag, to answer the call to patriotic duty. Appeals in varied media have been designed to reach people emotionally and to motivate them to act—join the military or take part in home-front activities that support armed conflict. At the same time, propaganda has urged antiwar protests. Just as there are calls to support war, there are opponents who exercise their right in a democracy to patriotic dissent. Both sides have expressed themselves from the Revolutionary War to this day.

In 1776, Thomas Paine, whose "Common Sense" pamphlet prompted many colonists to join the fight for independence, wrote a series of essays supporting a self-governing America. In one early essay, he declares: "These are the times that try men's souls. The summer soldier and the sunshine patriot will, in this crisis, shrink from the service of their country; but he that stands by it now, deserves the love and thanks of man and woman."[9]

Nevertheless, about a third to one half of the colonists (called Loyalists or Tories) were opposed to war against the British. Their reasons varied. Some could see no point in abandoning a monarchy that had existed for hundreds of years. Others were recent immigrants loyal to their homeland, or they were descendants of British citizens. About 100,000 fled to Canada, the Caribbean, or Florida (then under Spanish rule) or returned to England rather than take sides during the Revolutionary War. They also wanted to escape the zealous patriotism of rebels that frequently led to persecution. For example, loyalist Elizabeth Lichtenstein Johnston, who was a teenager at the time of the war, recalled the fate of some Tories in Georgia:

> If a Tory refused to join the people, he was imprisoned, and tarred and feathered. This was a terrible indignity, the poor creature being stripped naked, tarred all over, and then rolled in feathers. I might once, if I would have gone to the window, have seen a poor man carried all over the town with a mob around him, in such a plight, but the idea was too dreadful. He was an inoffensive man.[10]

From the time the United States entered World War I in 1917 to the end of the war, propaganda messages supporting U.S. involvement were widespread, although thousands did protest the draft. Emma Goldman, a Russian immigrant and radical political activist, made speeches across the nation criticizing involuntary military service. In one passionate speech, she said, "We, who came from Europe, came here looking to America as the promised land. I came believing that liberty was a fact. And when we today resent war and conscription, it is not that we are foreigners and don't care, it is precisely because we love America and we are opposed to war."[11] The federal government had no patience with protestors like Goldman. She was arrested and charged with breaking a new law that made antidraft activities a conspiracy against the federal government. After serving two years in jail, she was deported to Russia.

To reinforce support for the world war, various public and private agencies used posters to recruit soldiers, sailors, and workers for wartime industries. Posters encouraged conservation and fund raising. Artists who created the graphics worked for and with the government and the Division of Pictorial Publicity of the Committee of Public Information. One of those artists was James Montgomery Flagg, who created the famous Uncle Sam image pointing a finger with the words "I Want You for the U.S. Army." Other poster messages included "First Call. I need *you* in the *Navy* this minute! Our country will always be proudest of those who answered the *first call*"; "Be Patriotic. Sign your country's pledge to save the food"; "Women! Help America's sons win the war. Buy U.S. government bonds 2nd Liberty Loan of 1917"; "Halt the Hun! [a term for Germans]." According to Libby Chenault, University of North Carolina at Chapel Hill, "In just two years, America printed more than twenty million copies of perhaps 2,500 posters in support of the war effort."[12] Dr. Chenault points out:

> Making dramatic use of emotion-laden symbols such as the American flag, the Statue of Liberty, and Uncle Sam, these posters served as a call to action when democracy was in peril and reinforced an American's pride in country and his or her innate patriotism and readiness for sacrifice. Such posters also had the psychological importance of bringing the war home to the civilians and suggesting relatively small but meaningful sacrifices on their part.[13]

Posters also were effective in World War II propaganda. They frequently exhorted people to buy war bonds—"Buy a share of America." Posters issued warnings, such as the necessity of keeping quiet about U.S. military powers. For example: "Loose lips sink ships," "Loose talk can cost lives," "Somebody blabbed—button your lip!" and "A careless word, a needless sinking."

World War II print and broadcast media urged citizens to demonstrate their patriotism by planting "victory gardens" and canning fruits and vegetables so that agricultural production could provide for the armed forces overseas. The federal government also initiated rationing. The purpose was "to secure a fair distribution of scarce commodities," U.S. ration books stated, adding, "Getting along with less is part of your contribution to the war effort."[14] Sugar was the first product to be rationed, followed by coffee. Other items rationed included automobiles, tires, fuel oil, gasoline, meats and fats, processed foods, and shoes.

For the most part, Americans answered positively to propaganda supporting the "Good War," as it has been called. It was the "only major war that lacked an organized bloc of dissenters," writes David Greenberg for *Slate*. He explains, "Pearl Harbor had made an isolationist stance untenable, and as Americans learned more and more about Nazi Germany,

A sample ration book used by civilians during World War II. Photo by the author.

most anti-war activists decided the defeat of fascism was worth fighting for."[15]

"UNITED WE STAND?"

Appeals for support during the conflict in Vietnam proved to be more controversial and eventually less effective than other propaganda efforts for war. As the RAND Corporation puts it:

> The largest and perhaps least successful propaganda campaign in U.S. history was the "hearts and minds" information operation in Vietnam. . . . The two goals of U.S. propaganda operations in Vietnam were to undermine support of the Communist regime in North Vietnam and to solidify support for a pro-American South Vietnam. Despite enormous efforts, analysts at the RAND Corp. concluded in a 1970 report to the Pentagon that neither military actions nor propaganda operations could dent the morale and motivation of Communist forces.[16]

The failure of the Vietnam propaganda effort was only one of the varied factors that turned Americans against the war. Among them were the scenes shown on television news broadcasts that brought the reality of war home. Negative images included pictures of children fleeing napalm bombs, a prisoner being shot in the head, and coffins of American soldiers being shipped from Vietnam. The reinstitution of the draft also fueled antiwar sentiment, which was expressed frequently in

WHAT'S YOUR OPINION?

Many schools in the nation start each day with the Pledge of Allegiance to the U.S. flag. No one is forced to recite the pledge, however students usually stand as a sign of respect. But suppose a student or group of students refuses to stand as a way to protest an unjust act or a denial of a person's rights? Would such a student action be unpatriotic and disrespectful? What do you think?

PATRIOTIC MUSIC

From drum-and-fife music played by young boys as they marched with militia into revolutionary battle to the present military marching bands, national holiday parades, and sing alongs, music has stirred Americans' patriotic spirit. Most Americans are familiar with the national anthem, but 61 percent of 2,200 people 18 years of age and older did not know all of the words to the first verse, according to a 2004 Harris poll. An ABC news poll found that one in three teenagers does not know the name of the anthem—"The Star Spangled Banner"—and only 15 percent know the lyrics from memory. Thirty-five percent of teens surveyed knew Francis Scott Key wrote the words.[17] The National Association for Music Education launched a project to rekindle interest in the anthem; it culminated in mid-2007 with a record-setting concert featuring "The Star Spangled Banner." The anthem is musically complex and difficult for most singers to perform, yet it is played and sung across the land at events ranging from ball games to political rallies.

A much older patriotic musical rendition is "Yankee Doodle Dandy," a comic song and parody written in colonial times. According to the Library of Congress, the term *doodle* referred to a "fool or simpleton," while *dandy* described a "gentleman of affected manners, dress, and hairstyle. . . . Indeed, the British made fun of rag-tag American militiamen by playing 'Yankee Doodle' even as they headed toward the Battle of Lexington and Concord. . . . 'Yankee Doodle' has survived as one of America's most upbeat and humorous national airs."[18]

Dozens of other patriotic numbers have become part of the nation's heritage and include official songs of the Army, Navy, Marines, Air Force, and Coast Guard. Other familiar titles are "God Bless America," which is often called a second national anthem and was composed by Irving Berlin in 1938; "America (My Country 'tis of Thee)"; "America the Beautiful"; and "You're a Grand Old Flag." Folk songs also have expressed patriotism, such as Woody Guthrie's "This Land Is Your Land" written in 1940 and Lee Greenwood's "God Bless the USA" written in the 1980s, but have become widely popular since the September 11, 2001, attacks and the U.S. retaliation in Iraq.

The Library of Congress sums up patriotic music this way: "A combination of hymns, national songs, music of the theater, radio and television, military themes, and poetry, all of this music demonstrates that while over history many things have changed, this expression of pride and hope remain a constant part of the American experience."[19]

19

student protest demonstrations that occurred from the late 1960s to 1973, when the draft ended. Even after that, there were protests against voluntary service. A common refrain was "Hell no we won't go!"

Countless times the propaganda for and against Vietnam has been compared to the support and opposition to the war in Iraq. Propaganda slogans backing the Iraq War include "Fighting for our freedom," "Freedom is not free," "God bless America," "Support our troops," and "United we stand." Columnists, politicians, and others have berated protestors by calling them irresponsible, cowardly, unpatriotic, and treasonous. On the other side, posters and signs have read "No allegiance to war, torture and lies," "Not in our name and with our money," "Stop the war," "Thou shalt not kill children," and "We the people say *no*." And protestors have declared the war unwinnable, a mistake, criminal, based on lies, and an occupation of a nation.

Whichever side a person takes in wartime propaganda campaigns, the fact remains that Americans have the freedom to determine for themselves where they personally stand regarding war. They also have the right to express their patriotism, whether it is in dissent or in line with government views. In an essay for *Teen Ink*, Mike puts it this way: "Patriotism, to me, means for someone to do as much as they can to improve their country, even when it means opposing one's government, or the actions or beliefs of a majority of its citizens."[20]

NOTES

1. Bonnie K., "In the Name of Patriotism," *Teen Ink*, May 2006, teenink.com/Past/2006/May/20211.html (accessed June 23, 2007).

2. "Flagship Study of America's Youth Describes What Teens Want," Press Release, Harrison Group, November 2006, www.harrisongroupinc.com/index.php?q=node/57 (accessed June 23, 2007).

3. Bonnie K., "In the Name of Patriotism."

4. Quoted in Marti Attoun, "Sacred Duty," *American Profile.com*, October 30, 2005, www.americanprofile.com/article/4996.html (accessed June 23, 2007).

5. Mayor Ross C. "Rocky" Anderson, Address, Washington Square, Salt Lake City, Utah, August 30, 2006, www.ci.slc.ut.us/mayor/speeches/2006%20speeches/SPdemonstration83006.pdf (accessed June 23, 2007).

6. Anderson, Address.

7. Anderson, Address.

8. "Vice President's Remarks at a Rally for the Indiana Air and Army National Guard," Press Release, Office of the Vice President, October 20, 2006, www.whitehouse.gov/news/releases/2006/10/20061020-3.html (accessed June 23, 2007).

9. Thomas Paine, "The Crisis," Independence Hall Association, December 23, 1776, 12.164.81.10/paine/index.htm (accessed June 24, 2007).

10. Elizabeth Lichtenstein Johnston, *Recollections of a Georgia Loyalist Written in 1836*, ed. Rev. Arthur Wentworth Eaton (London: M. F. Mansfield, 1901), p. 44.

11. Quoted in Candace Serena Falk, *Love, Anarchy, and Emma Goldman* (New York: Holt, Rinehart, and Winston, 1984; reprint, New Brunswick, NJ: Rutgers University Press, 1990), p. 156.

12. Libby Chenault, "American Posters of the Great War," *Documenting the American South*, 2004, docsouth.unc.edu/wwi/postersintro.html (accessed June 23, 2007).

13. Chenault, "American Posters of the Great War."

14. United States of America Office of Price Administration, U.S. Ration Books, 1943.

15. David Greenberg, "Advise and Dissent: How Anti-War Protest Movements Have Made the U.S. Stronger," *Slate.com*, March 26, 2003, www.slate.com/id/2080735 (accessed June 23, 2007).

16. Lowell Schwartz, "War, Propaganda and Public Opinion," first appeared in *Baltimore Sun*, December 18, 2005, www.rand.org/commentary/121805BS.html (accessed June 23, 2007).

17. "Has America Lost Its Voice?" The National Anthem Project, January 18, 2007, www.thenationalanthemproject.org/factsheet.html (accessed June 23, 2007). See also Samantha L. Quigley, "Project to Rekindle Singing of National Anthem,"

American Forces Information Service, U.S. Department of Defense, November 5, 2005, www.defenselink.mil/news/Nov2004/ n11052004_2004110507.html (accessed June 23, 2007).

18. "Patriotic Melodies," Library of Congress Music Division, n.d., memory.loc.gov/cocoon/ihas/loc.natlib.ihas.200000025/ default.html (accessed February 9, 2007).

19. "Patriotic Melodies."

20. Mike M., "Complacency and the False Patriotism," *Teen Ink*, December 2002, teenink.com/Past/2002/December/Opinion/Complacency.html (accessed June 23, 2007).

To Serve or Not to Serve?

For seventeen-year-old Isaac Miguel of Honolulu, Hawaii, making the choice to serve was and is a patriotic duty and his "first grown-up decision."[2] He told a reporter, "I still needed my parents' permission, but I wanted to do something different, something bigger than myself."[3] That "something" was signing up for the U.S. Marine Corps in early 2007. He said, "I felt the sense that I needed to pay back my country."[4] Patriotism is a primary motivation for many students who enlist in the military. They frequently say that their country has given them everything, so they want to repay that debt. Seventeen-year-old Brett Goldizen of Perry Village, Ohio, joined the Marine Corps in early 2007 because he "was attracted to the overall values the Marine Corps stands for: the discipline, honor, courage, commitment and physical aspects of it."[5] Many young people choose a military service career for educational and travel opportunities. A graduate of St. John–Endicott High School in Idaho, nineteen-year-old Brent Mansell needed money for college and joined the Coast Guard, which had been his plan since grade school.

Yet, as previously noted, numerous teens do not want to be part of the armed forces, and frequently their opposition to military life is based on the involvement of the United States in the Iraq conflict. In February 2007, for example, students at the University of California, Santa Barbara and Santa Cruz, as well as at Columbia in New York City organized one-day strikes against the war. As a form of protest, the students refused to go to class or to work or shop. Other protests

"Make the choice to serve in a cause larger than your wants."

—President George W. Bush addressing young people at his inauguration in 2005[1]

across the United States have included antirecruiting campaigns at military recruitment centers and at high school and college campuses. Since 2003, tactics to protest military recruitment at the University of Kansas in Lawrence, for instance, have involved lectures, panel discussions, sign displays, and occupation of recruitment offices.

On the other hand, some students welcome recruiters. One who received fairly wide acceptance was volunteer recruiter Evie Alexopoulos, a West Point graduate, former army first lieutenant, and winner of the Mrs. Florida Pageant. She believes girls should join the army and wants to destroy the concept that women in the military are plain and unfeminine. She told Tampa, Florida, high school girls, "You can be glamorous and graceful and be a trained killer behind the scenes. And you can be a mother and a daughter" and still be part of the military.[6] Students were impressed with her message, and several asked for her autograph, which she signed on the back of a professional recruiter's business card.

RECRUITMENT

"The ability to acquire sufficient quantities of high-quality U.S. Army personnel has been imperative since World War II, when the United States became a superpower with global security responsibilities," writes Col. John M. Collins (ret.).[7] He points out in the 2005 edition of *AUSA: Army Magazine* that "many eligible U.S. youths" are reluctant to join the armed forces because of the struggle against unpredictable terrorists.[8] His view has been echoed by other military officers. Nevertheless, some officials and recruiters say that recruitment for active duty in the army was up in 2006, although its reserve units were short of enlistees.

To increase the number of recruits, the military uses such tools as a video game called *America's Army*, first released in 2002, with several new versions available in subsequent years. It's a multiplayer combat video game that a person can download free from the army's website. The game's development team surveyed enlistees at Fort Benning, Georgia, and found that "about 60 percent of recruits said they've played 'America's Army' more than five times a week. Four out of 100 said they'd joined the Army specifically because of the game," according to a 2006 report in the *Christian Science Monitor.*[9]

Recruiters also take advantage of paintball tournaments where many teenagers compete. In a paintball game, players wear padded shirts and helmets to protect themselves from capsules of nontoxic, water-soluble dye shot from gas-powered guns. Two teams try to steal each other's flag while protecting their own, and if a player is hit by a paintball he or she is out of the game. Because a paintball player learns such skills as marksmanship and how to escape "enemy" fire, recruiters could convince players that their skills can be transferred to the military.

To gain enlistees, recruiters may offer free iPods, prizes at sports competitions, sports gear like footballs and baseball caps, and T-shirts. Or they propose enlistment bonuses of $11,000 and up to $40,000 for qualified individuals in special services and $72,000 for college expenses, as of 2007.

Another strategy initiated in 2006 was designed to attract "highly-qualified individuals who might otherwise have been excluded from joining"[10] the armed forces because of the tattoos that adorn many youth today. Army Regulation 670-1 allows soldiers to have tattoos on the hands and back of the neck if they are not "extremist, indecent, sexist or racist."[11] The army has always banned indecent tattoos on any part of the body, and previously, tattoos were prohibited if they were not covered by a dress uniform. The change in the tattoo policy "was made because Army officials realized the number of potential recruits bearing skin art had grown enormously over the years," according to the Army News Service.[12]

Another method to boost recruitment has been to grant more waivers so that people who score poorly on aptitude tests or are high school dropouts as well as those who have criminal records can join the armed forces. After military officials scrutinize applicants and accept their community references, they may allow waivers for potential enlistees who

MILITARY TATTOOS

Who hasn't heard about or seen the popular cartoon character Popeye the sailorman with his anchor tattoo on his forearm? Cartoonist Elzie Segar (who died in 1938) created the Popeye character in 1929, and since then, the figure has appeared worldwide on objects ranging from animated toys to statues. The anchor tattoo has been embedded on the skin of many American sailors over the centuries. In fact, tattooing has a long tradition in the American military, although the beginnings of this art form date back thousands of years.

At the time of the American Revolution, sailors adopted a tattooing custom that had become widely popular in the British navy, and Americans frequently described their tattoos in diaries, journals, and letters. During the Civil War period in the 1860s, tattoos gained increased popularity among both the Union and Confederate troops. Many in the armed forces were tattooed by one of the first professional tattooists, a German immigrant named Martin Hildebrandt, who eventually set up shop in New York City in 1870.[13]

By the end of the 1800s, the Spanish-American War of 1898 prompted numerous tattoos. The war began after a mysterious explosion sunk the USS *Maine*, killing 260 sailors onboard. U.S. government officials blamed Spain for the disaster, although there was no proof the nation planned the attack, but the war cry that evolved was "Remember the Maine, to hell with Spain!" and as Terisa Green writes, "sailors of the era rushed in droves to have it tattooed on their chests before heading out to avenge her sinking."[14]

The World War II era—sometimes called the "golden age of tattooing"—brought another resurgence of tattooed service members. Tattoo shops were located close to ports or military bases. Sailors and soldiers commonly had the names of their ships, divisions, or battlefields tattooed on their bodies. Tattoos of naked women were also popular, but these were prohibited in the navy, so such tattoos had to be reinked, adding some type of clothing to the bodies.

In modern times, military tattoos frequently show allegiance to a particular branch of service or are general patriotic symbols such as an American flag, the Statue of Liberty, eagles, banners with *freedom* inscribed, and stars and stripes in various forms. A popular military tattoo that originated during World War II is still prevalent today: soldiers raising the American flag in Iwo Jima.

have committed felonies, misdemeanors, or drug offenses, usually at a young age. Such waivers (called moral waivers, differentiated from medical waivers for health problems) have increased from 4,918 in 2003 to 8,129 in 2006, according to Pentagon data.[15] Critics charge that felons could be a detriment in the armed forces and endanger others on the battlefield. Military officials defend the waivers program, arguing that ex-offenders deserve a second chance and that military service often helps with rehabilitation.

SCHOOL RECRUITMENT

Rural areas and secondary schools and colleges are considered the best places for recruitment. But recruitment practices have become a contentious issue, particularly since the Elementary and Secondary Education Act, also known as the No Child Left Behind Act (NCLB), became law in 2002. NCLB was established to improve America's public schools by setting high standards and ensuring that students, regardless of their background or ability, have well-prepared teachers, research-based curricula, and safe schools. But one part of the law's 670 pages is Section 9258 (beginning on page 559), with the heading "Armed Forces Recruiter Access to Students and Student Recruiting Information." It states that

> each local educational agency receiving assistance under this Act shall provide, on a request made by military recruiters or an institution of higher education, access to secondary school students names, addresses, and telephone listings.
>
> A secondary school student or the parent of the student may request that the student's name, address, and telephone listing . . . not be released without prior written parental consent, and the local educational agency or private school shall notify parents of the option to make a request and shall comply with any request.
>
> Each local educational agency receiving assistance under this Act shall provide military recruiters the same access to secondary school students as is provided generally to

post-secondary educational institutions or to prospective employers of those students.

The requirements of this section do not apply to a private secondary school that maintains a religious objection.[16]

If schools do not comply with the act, they will lose millions in federal funding. Since the beginning of the Iraq war, the number of students who have requested that they not be contacted by the military has grown. To opt out of providing information to the military, a student or parent must check off a form or sign a letter, which is provided as part of a student handbook, mailed to parents, or sent home with students. Also, antiwar groups may distribute pamphlets that include opt-out forms. Some are available on the Internet and can be found with the search term "opt-out forms." These forms have to be returned to the school administration office.

In some cases, students and their parents are not aware of what is in a student handbook or do not pay close attention to information regarding the NCLB Act. Michigan teenager Brittany Jones, who regularly writes for a teen blog on battlecreekenquirer.com, noted: "I never knew that letter [about NCLB] or even this whole issue existed. What high school student sits down and reads their handbook? Certainly not too many of us do. But how are we students supposed to have our parents sign that letter if we do not even know that it exists?" She suggested that a better way to inform parents and students was to put information "in the school newsletter for parents and students to read. Or just at least have our teachers go over it in the handbook."[17]

Other high school students have taken notice of the NCLB and the forms to opt out. For example, at Stevenson High School in a suburb of Chicago, Illinois, more than 50 percent of the nearly 4,500 students have completed and submitted the forms.[18] Near the end of 2005, the *Boston Globe* reported that in Massachusetts, "more than 5,000 high school students in five of the state's largest school districts have removed their names from military recruitment lists. . . . Overall, approximately 18 percent of the public high school students eligible in Cambridge, Boston, Worcester, Lowell, and Fall River have opted to remove their names."[19]

Similar opt-out situations exist in high schools across the United States, but in spite of the opt-out choice, recruiters still focus on school campuses because they can reach a large group of potential recruits. This reduces the costs of promoting the military and helps recruiters meet their goals. Recruiters also have many opportunities to meet with and talk to students at community events, the mall, or other public places. They often tell students that because their nation is at war, the country needs smart, hard-working students to join the army.

Recruiters also can call or visit students at home, acquiring names and addresses from such sources as job fairs, career days, or Internet queries for information about the armed forces. Some students have no objection to military recruiters being on school campuses or contacting them. As one senior at a San Diego, California, high school noted during an interview for a PBS program, there was no pressure by recruiters to sign up for the military. Another student said recruiters are "not here to force us to join. They're just giving us an idea of, like, what you get in the Army." A third teenager declared, "I don't feel any need to go and sign up for the Army. This is just helping us open up our options about what we want to do later in life."[20]

THE SOLOMON AMENDMENT

Just as the NCLB Act cuts off federal funds to secondary schools that do not meet military access guidelines, so the Solomon Amendment denies federal funding to colleges and universities that prohibit or prevent Reserve Officer Training Corp (ROTC) programs or military recruitment on campus. The Solomon Amendment, named for the late U.S. Representative Gerald Solomon of New York, is a federal law first enacted in the 1990s as part of the National Defense Authorization Act, and it has been revised several times since.

In 2001, the amendment was altered to block federal funds to universities that did not allow recruiters on campus. The modification was aimed primarily at law schools, which had tried and failed to get the military to discard its "Don't Ask, Don't Tell" policy. That policy bars openly gay people from military service. Law schools wanted to make it difficult for the military to recruit, so they required all employers (including the military) to sign a pledge not to discriminate on the basis of sexual orientation if they wanted to use school facilities for interviews. The U.S. Congress refused to accept these conditions and instead passed more rigid legislation that cut off federal funds to entire universities where military recruiting was banned.

In 2003, law professors and students represented by the Forum for Academic and Institutional Rights (FAIR) challenged the law in court. FAIR argued that the military rule violated its members' First Amendment freedoms of speech and association and the nondiscrimination policies of the schools. With military recruiters on campus, the schools were being forced to disseminate a message of support for the "Don't Ask" policy. FAIR also argued that they were being compelled to present the military view that openly homosexual individuals were unfit for the armed forces.

Although a federal circuit court ruled in FAIR's favor, the case was appealed to the U.S. Supreme Court in *Rumsfeld, Secretary of Defense, et al. v. Forum for Academic and Institutional Rights, Inc., et al.* (*Rumsfeld v. FAIR*). In an 8–0 decision (Justice Alito did not participate because he was not on the bench when the case was argued), the High Court determined in 2006 that the

> students and faculty are free to associate to voice their disapproval of the military's message; nothing about the statute affects the composition of the group by making group membership less desirable. The Solomon Amendment therefore does not violate a law school's First Amendment rights. A military recruiter's mere presence on campus does not violate a law school's right to associate, regardless of how repugnant the law school considers the recruiter's message.[21]

The Supreme Court thus reversed the circuit court's decision.

REINSTATING THE DRAFT?

The military draft was suspended in 1973, but since then, debates over whether conscription should be reinstated have emerged on occasion. After the United States sent armed forces into Iraq, rumors circulated on the Internet, in classrooms, and through published news stories that the government would or was taking steps to restore the draft. While legislation has been proposed in Congress to do just that, there has been very little support for passage. Still, the pros and cons of a draft are argued, particularly among young adults who would be affected the most.

For instance, in 2004 on the *Village Voice* website, twenty-one-year-old Karl posted this comment: "I don't think [a draft is] necessary. I think there is still enough interest in the volunteer army. . . . I think I would go if I were drafted, but I like to think I would enlist first." In the opinion of teenager Ken Wee, a draft would "be a good idea. Other countries have a draft and it makes [people] better citizens. But I don't think this country would go for it." A different view came from twenty-year-old Sophie: "I would avoid [a draft] as much as possible. I don't support a draft at all. But at the same time, I'd be against any loopholes, even for women. Everyone should have to go or not go equally." Wrote another young woman: "I just don't think it's right to force people to go to war." And Kya, who was twenty-one at the time, noted: "All hell would break loose. Maybe it would mobilize the anti-war movement, though. Maybe the resistance would be greater."[22]

While a majority of Americans (including high school students) opposes a military draft, students in several Austin, Texas, high schools wrote anonymous comments in a 2005 survey that indicated some support for conscription. As one student at Westlake High School responded: "I would not want a draft implemented, but if one was, I would openly support it and willingly fight for my country." Another Westlake student wrote, "I believe the draft is a good idea because that way everyone serves their country." Wrote another: "I would be completely fine with a draft. I am already going to join the military after high school."[23] At Reagan High School in Austin, a student supported the draft "as long as rich people get drafted." One more high-schooler thought the Iraq War would "end quicker" with a draft.[24]

NOTES

1. George W. Bush, Press Release, The White House, January 20, 2005, www.whitehouse.gov/news/releases/2005/01/20050120-1 .html (accessed April 22, 2007).

2. Quoted in Leland Kim, "Local Teen Answers a Call to Duty," KHNL NBC 8, January 10, 2007, www.khnl.com/Global/ story.asp?S=5916927&nav=menu55_1 (accessed June 23, 2007).

3. Quoted in Kim, "Local Teen Answers a Call to Duty."

4. Quoted in Kim, "Local Teen Answers a Call to Duty."

5. Quoted in Mark Tuscano, "Calling the Few, the Proud," *News-Herald.com*, February 7, 2007, www.zwire.com/site/news.cfm ?newsid=17818769&BRD=1698&PAG=461&dept_id=21849&rfi=6 (accessed June 23, 2007).

6. Quoted in Justin George, "Not Your Ordinary Military Recruiter," *St. Petersburg Times*, February 6, 2006, Section B, p. 1.

7. Col. John M. Collins, USA Ret., "Army Recruiting Crisis: Problems, Responses and Prognosis," *AUSA: Army Magazine*, August 1, 2005, www.ausa.org/webpub/DeptArmyMagazine.nsf/ byid/KGRG-6EWRMU (accessed June 24, 2007).

8. Collins, "Army Recruiting Crisis."

9. Patrick Jonnson, "Enjoy the Video Game? Then Join the Army," *Christian Science Monitor*, September 19, 2006, www.csmonitor.com/2006/0919/p01s04-usmi.html (accessed June 23, 2007).

10. J. D. Leipold, "Army Changes Tattoo Policy," Army News Service, March 15, 2006, www4.army.mil/ocpa/read.php?story_id_ key=8692 (accessed June 23, 2007).

11. Leipold, "Army Changes Tattoo Policy."

12. Leipold, "Army Changes Tattoo Policy."

13. Kathlyn Gay and Christine Whittington, *Body Marks: Tattooing, Piercing, and Scarification* (Brookfield, CT: Twenty-First Century Books, 2002), pp. 7, 31.

14. Terisa Green, "More Than Skin Deep," *The American Legion*, December 2003, p. 34.

15. Lizette Alvarez, "Army Giving More Waivers in Recruiting," *New York Times*, February 14, 2007, www.nytimes.com/2007/02/14/us/14military.html?hp&ex=11715156 00&en=d763ab40cba3657d&ei=5094&partner=homepage (accessed June 23, 2007); see also Mark Thompson, "Lowering the Recruiting Standards?" *Time*, February 14, 2007, www.time.com/

time/nation/article/0,8599,1589745,00.html (accessed June 23, 2007); Michael Boucai, J.D., *"Balancing Your Strengths against Your Felonies": Considerations for Military Recruitment of Ex-Offenders*, Whitepaper, February 2007, www.palmcenter.org/publications/dadt/balancing_your_strengths_against_your_felonies (accessed June 23, 2007).

16. Public Law 107-110, January 8, 2002, www.ed.gov/policy/elsec/leg/esea02/107-110.pdf (accessed June 23, 2007).

17. Brittany Jones, "Students Need to Be Aware of Where Their Information Goes," *Battle Creek Enquirer Fresh Voices*, February 18, 2007, noise.typepad.com/youth_blog/2007/02/students_need_t.html (accessed June 16, 2007).

18. Judy Keen, "Some Opt Out of Military Options," *USA Today*, November 4, 2006, www.usatoday.com/news/education/2006-11-02-recruits_x.htm (accessed June 23, 2007).

19. Maria Sacchetti and Jenna Russell, "Students Rebuffing Military Recruiters," *Boston.com*, November 13, 2005, www.boston.com/news/education/k_12/articles/2005/11/13/students_rebuffing_military_recruiters (accessed June 23, 2007).

20. John Merrow, interviewer, "High School Recruiting," PBS *Newshour*, December 13, 2004, www.pbs.org/newshour/bb/military/july-dec04/recruit_12-13.html (accessed June 16, 2007).

21. U.S. Supreme Court, *Rumsfeld, Secretary of Defense, et al. v. Forum for Academic and Institutional Rights, Inc., et al.*, argued December 6, 2005; decided March 6, 2006, www.supremecourtus.gov/opinions/05pdf/04-1152.pdf (accessed June 23, 2007).

22. Ta-Nehisi Coates, "Old Enough to Vote? Old Enough to Die," *Village Voice*, May 4, 2004, www.villagevoice.com/news/0418,coates,53196,1.html (accessed June 23, 2007).

23. Nonmilitary Options for Youth, "Survey Responses, Westlake High School," October 20, 2005, www.progressiveaustin.org/nmofy/drupal//?q=node/86 (accessed June 16, 2007).

24. Nonmilitary Options for Youth, "Survey Results, Reagan HS," March 24, 2005, www.progressiveaustin.org/nmofy/drupal//?q=node/23 (accessed June 16, 2007).

"Journey of Self-Discovery"

"Basic Combat Training (BCT) is a training course that transforms civilians into Soldiers"[2] is the first sentence on a U.S. Army website that explains what is officially known as initial-entry training. The site includes descriptions of what to expect for each week in the "journey of self-discovery," as the army calls it.[3]

Each branch of service maintains its own website with information about training. The U.S. Marine Corps, for example, greets anyone who accesses its site with "Marine

"We all lined up, and we were all given specific instructions, but some of the recruits messed it up, so they got their butts chewed, big time."

—eighteen-year-old navy recruit[1]

DID YOU KNOW?

The term *boot camp* originated during the Spanish-American War of 1898. Sailors wore leggings called boots, and the practice continued for new inductees through World War II. The term *boot* came to mean a recruit who received his basic training at "boot camps."[4] He had to wear the white canvas leggings that were twelve inches high, with eyelets and laces that tightly secured the leggings over bell-bottom pants. The leggings were connected by straps and buckles to polished black shoes.

Sgt. First Class James Youngdahl calls cadence as he brings new recruits from the Recruit Sustainment Program back in from a one-mile run during drill assembly in 2005. Photo courtesy U.S. Army.

OFF THE SHELF

Books about basic training are available at most book stores or at online websites. Some examples of titles include:

- *The Ultimate Basic Training Guidebook* by Michael Volkin;
- *Army Basic Training: Be Smart, Be Ready* by Raquel D. Thiebes;
- *The Real Insider's Guide to Military Basic* by Peter Thompson;
- *Guide to Joining the Military: Air Force—Army—Coast Guard—Marine Corps—Navy* by Scott A. Ostrow; and
- *Honor, Courage, Commitment: Navy Boot Camp* by J. F. Leahy.

Corps Recruit Training is meant to separate those capable of being Marines from those who are not."[5] Boot camp is what the U.S. Navy calls its basic training: "This is where the amazing Navy transformation from civilian to Sailor happens . . . 8 weeks of mental and physical training. Expect it to be rigorous and demanding. It's hard work. Then again, anything worth something usually is."[6] You can find similar greetings and information about basic training at the official sites for the U.S. Air Force and the U.S. Coast Guard.[7] (The latter is part of the U.S. Department of Homeland Security.) In addition, pamphlets about each branch of service are available to download, and Internet forums by and for military personnel provide a look at real recruits' experiences. Also, dozens of commercial books on basic training have been published in recent years.

HOW PAST RECRUITS TRAINED

Although military training has changed over the years along with new technologies, weapons, airplanes, and other matériel, some of the practices that have been used continuously to ready recruits for armed conflict include drills, marches, combat exercises, and inspections. From handwritten diaries and letters of earlier wars to Internet communication today, recruits' messages have described their training procedures.

During the Revolutionary War, the War of 1812, and through the Civil War, troops had very little preparation for warfare. Those who fought in the Revolution usually were members of a militia, and many were rural folks who were hunters and with one shot could kill animals for food. Thus they were expected to use that skill to destroy the enemy.

During the Civil War, soldiers might serve only a few months, and training often consisted of learning to use a gun and marching in parade, a form of discipline. One young Civil War inductee, John Dunipace, in a letter to a cousin noted that he had a "good drillmaster" who thought "the boys learn fast. . . . We have dress parade every night and we have to drill one hour in the forenoon and one-hour after supper and the noncommissioned officers drill at 2 o'clock and we are on duty every three days."[8]

Drills and reviews were very much a part of World War I training, as shown in Ferris W. Myrice's diary, held at the Center for Archival Collections at Bowling Green (Ohio) State University. After enlistment, Myrice was sent to Camp Sherman in Ohio, northwest of Chillicothe. The camp was known as the "Soldier Factory" because thousands of U.S. Army troops were trained there in 1917 and 1918. Myrice's diary begins with his enlistment on March 28, 1918. Some of his entries (with his spelling and punctuation) appear here:

> **March 29.** Arrived at Camp Sherman. . . . Drill and detail work. . . .
> **April 21.** Practiced sighting all day. Received Rifle belt, bayonet, pack etc.
> **April 26.** . . . left for 5 days on the rifle range. Some experience work from 5 A.M. until 8 P.M. every day . . . very realistic at retreat when the band played "Star S.B." and they were having rapid firing practice in the range.
> **May 3.** First day at bombing and bayonets drill.
> **May 4.** Learning to pitch tents.
> **May 5.** Passed in Review. . . . Heaps of fun getting ready for bunk inspection—changed model for equipment six times.
> **May 12.** Visitors galore—Received my first pass. . . .
> **May 13.** Started gas drill night hike of 8 miles
> **May 15.** Big day—on kitchen police—pay day and entered the gas chamber in gas drill [to counter poison gas].
> **May 19.** Skermish drill on the range. hiked out and in on Sunday.[9]

Myrice's diary continued with descriptions of his transfer to New York, shipping out in June for Europe, and observations of conditions there through the end of July. Bill, another World War I enlistee, sent a postcard with a short summary of his training: "From 7:30 to 10:45 we have infantry drill, bayonet drill and physical exercise. That doesn't mean 5 minutes drill and rest either . . . A total 20 minutes rest in that time. We generally have . . . combat problems between 1:00

and 4:00 pm rain, mud or dust. . . . [Then] 28 inch steps at 140 steps per [minute] on a hike of several miles."[10]

When World War II erupted, training had to be adapted to the new types of warfare. Byron Armbruster enlisted in the army in 1942 and reported: "Besides our regular training, laying tank mines, building barbed wire barricades, close drill and extended drill, we have been taking five mile marches with packs and rifles on our backs. These marches will be increased and next week we are expected to go twenty miles in ten hours."[11] William Sprague was a high school senior in 1941 when the United States entered World War II. He enlisted in the U.S. Coast Guard in 1942 and in later years wrote a memoir of his time in the military. The memoir was posted on a Coast Guard history website and includes a look at his boot camp experiences that were a mixture of

> calisthenics, marching, manual of arms, muscle racking tetanus shots and scrubbing decks and clothes. . . . Discipline was strict and the schedule tight. Reveille at 5:30. Dressed and formed up on the company street by 6:00 for calisthenics. 6:30 to 6:45 make sure your bunk was properly made up and fall in again on the company street to be marched to the mess hall for breakfast. At 7:30 the daily training routine started and lasted until about 5:00 in the afternoon. After the day's routine of training we were on free time unless you had drawn guard duty.
>
> One of the skills that was required of us to learn was the manual of arms. This is a series of actions that are performed with a rifle and must be done precisely and on commands given by the drill master. Toward the end of boot camp they would have what was called a knock-out drill. The entire company would line up on the parade ground, complete with wooden rifles, and be put through the manual of arms. If you made a mistake, you were knocked out and the person who ended up on the parade ground alone was the winner and was awarded an overnight liberty.[12]

Another World War II Coast Guard enlistee was Donna Ione Smith, who joined the service after graduating from high school. At the time, the Coast Guard started the women's

Arthur Gay, World War II sailor in uniform in 1943. Photo courtesy Arthur Gay.

One of the duties for recruits in the U.S. Navy is scrubbing down the deck, as shown in this photo of a Korean War enlistee, the late Dean Hamilton. Photo courtesy Karen Hamilton.

Dean Hamilton in uniform. Photo courtesy Karen Hamilton.

reserve called Semper Paratus/Always Ready (SPARS; semper paratus is the Coast Guard motto and title of its song). Smith received her training at Oklahoma Agricultural and Mechanical College (A&M), which is now Oklahoma State University. She told an interviewer for a Coast Guard oral history program, "I was trained as a yeoman [a petty officer assigned to administrative duties]," adding "we really studied hard . . . and we did learn a lot. So it was not only about the training itself, but about the service and what was expected of us and everything. But at that particular time, of course, the women were to take the place of men so men could go overseas. . . . So we were mainly to go to, like, headquarters or offices."[13]

MODERN RECRUITS

According to the U.S. Army Training and Doctrine Command (TRADOC), "Gone are the days when recruits arrived at basic training to learn just the fundamentals of weaponry, how to fight from a foxhole, how to march in parade formations and a mere three days in the field. In those days prior to 2003, TRADOC gave recruits nut-and-bolt basics, then sent the new Soldiers to their units where the real training started."[14] Since 2003, recruits are in the field for twenty-one days during the training period to learn intensive combat skills. They take part in a "weapons immersion" program, receiving their weapon three days after they arrive. They carry their weapon "to the dining facility, clear it before entering and do functions checks throughout the day," explains General William S. Wallace, TRADOC commander. He continues, "Instead of locking the weapon up in an arms room at night, they put it in a weapons rack in the barracks." General Wallace points out, "When you ask 100 young people how many of them have fired a weapon, you might get eight or 10 raised hands. They aren't familiar with weapons, which is good from a societal perspective but that's not necessarily a good thing from a military perspective. So we've got to teach them how to use their weapons and how to be comfortable with them."[15]

The general's words barely touch on what is actually involved in basic training, especially from a recruit's standpoint. In a series of ten articles posted on the TRADOC website in 2004, reporter Fred Baker followed four recruits through their nine weeks of BCT at A Battery, First Battalion, Seventy-ninth Field Artillery (nicknamed Alphatraz), Fort Sill, Oklahoma. One of the trainees was teenager Austin Fay from Mississippi, who quit school to work odd jobs when his girlfriend became pregnant. He enlisted because he decided his army training would help him find a better way to support his soon-to-be family. He told Baker, "I'm only 17. It's hard to find a job at 17."[16] Fay's first days with his platoon included learning how to assemble his field gear, doing hundreds of push-ups, and saying countless times, "Yes, drill sergeant!" At the end of the week, he was asked what he missed most. The answer: "his fiancée, McDonald's and zippers." Why zippers? "It's hard to use the bathroom wearing all your gear." The reporter noted that it takes at least 10 minutes to remove gear and undo all of the buttons.[17]

As the weeks roll on, trainees are required to complete road marches—fifteen kilometers (nine miles) for the final

Drill Instructor Sgt. Robert Dona at the Marine Corps Recruit Depot, Parris Island, South Carolina, "encourages" Marine Corps recruits to "sound-off" during drill in 2005. Photo by Staff Sgt. Ken Tinnin, courtesy Marine Corps.

Along with learning how to wage war, recruits also quickly pick up the meanings of acronyms used throughout the army. A few examples follow:

ACU army combat uniform
ARM advanced rifle marksmanship
BAC bayonet assault course
BDE brigade
BN battalion
BRM basic rifle marksmanship
CO or **company** a BCT unit containing as many as 250 soldiers. (Several companies make up a battalion. Several battalions make up a brigade.)
COE the contemporary operating environment
FOB forward-operating base
FTC fitness training company
FTW the Fit-to-Win Course, a physically demanding layout of horizontal obstacles soldiers complete as a squad
FTX field training exercise
IN inspection
INF infantry
ITT individual tactical techniques
Land Nav land navigation
LES leave and earnings statement
MOPP mission-oriented protective posture (gas mask, chemical-protective overgarment, etc.)
MRE meal, ready to eat
NBC nuclear biological chemical training
NIC Night Infiltration Course
OCS Officer Candidate School
POV privately owned vehicle, not allowed for soldiers in BCT or Advanced Individual Training
PT physical training
REGT regiment
STX situational training exercise[18]

one—with rucksacks on their backs; go through the gas chamber to learn how to put on, clear, and seal their protective masks; scale up and rappel down the forty-foot high Treadmill Tower with its obstacles; practice use of the M-16 rifles; train in hand-to-hand combat; and set up and live at a forward-operating base in the field. There's also preparation for the army physical fitness test, which, along with qualifying with the M-16s and other tests, must be passed in order to graduate from BCT. Out of the 238 Fort Sill trainees whom reporter Baker followed, 181 made the grade and became new warriors—U.S. Army soldiers. An excited Pvt. Austin Fay told Baker: "I've been waiting for this for nine weeks now, and I did it. I told you I would [do it]. I told you I had to, and I did."[19]

NAVY BOOT CAMP

About 50,000 young men and women enlist each year in the navy. Making the transition from citizens to sailors begins at the U.S. Navy Recruit Training Command (NRTC) in Great Lakes, Illinois, the only boot camp training facility in the country. In 2000, one former navy man and retired business executive, J. F. Leahy, was allowed to interview and follow a division of navy enlistees, from the time the recruits gathered at Chicago's O'Hare Airport and traveled by bus to Great Lakes through their boot camp and graduation. They came from the East and West Coasts, southern and northern states, and the Midwest. Leahy recorded their experiences and remarks in *Honor, Courage, Commitment: Navy Boot Camp*, published in 2002. Some of the comments provide a brief look at enlistee reactions. Consider eighteen-year-old Ashleigh Pankratz from Montana who had just arrived at Great Lakes with other enlistees and was greeted by a petty officer barking orders. As she explained, "I was shaking at first, because this guy was just yelling at everybody."[20]

Among the eighteen chapters of Leahy's book, he details aspects of boot camp in such chapters as "Orientation"; "The Early Weeks of Training"; "The Right Way, the Wrong Way, the Navy Way"; "The Warrior Weeks"; and "Battle Stations! Fighting the Good Fight." During orientation, Leahy asked about the food served—navy food is supposed to be a notch above that of the other services. So what kind of responses did he get?

- "Navy food is no different from any other cafeteria food, I guess . . . tastes similar to lunchroom food when I was in school."

- "The food is good but not great."

- "I don't mind the Navy food at all."

- "They say the Navy has the best food of all the services. God help the Army and Air Force."[21]

Chapters on battle stations cover recruits' intensive testing to determine if they are prepared to join the fleet.

Since Leahy's book was published, the navy has developed a new trainer complex called Battle Stations 21, completed in 2007. The entertainment and theme park industries helped create modern special effects for the "virtual training" that takes place in a 157,000-square-foot building, which in itself is a simulator. When recruits enter the $82.5 million facility, they march to a pier that is a facsimile of an actual pier in Norfolk, Virginia. A replica of a guided-missile destroyer called the USS *Trayer* is docked, and 90,000 gallons of water splash alongside. Special effects at the site include sea and diesel scents as well as sounds and lighting that represent a realistic scene. Aboard the *Trayer*, recruits stow their gear and go through a grueling twelve-hour test of their problem-solving, communications, and other essential skills. The test occurs in simulated crisis situations (called scenarios). As the navy explains

U.S. Navy recruits stand at attention following the successful completion of battle stations, the final portion of navy recruit training, at Recruit Training Command, Great Lakes, Illinois, 2006. Department of Defense photo by Chief Petty Officer Johnny Bivera, U.S. Navy.

recruits will experience horrifying realism, from mass casualties to a burning ship. Among the touches, built-in MP3

> ## A REMARKABLE FACT!
>
> Can you imagine a naval training center in the middle of the country? That's where the Great Lakes Training Station was built in the early 1900s. Why would anyone even suggest a location a thousand miles from the ocean when there are huge naval stations on both coasts and in Hawaii?
>
> In the past, when sailors enlisted in the navy, they went directly to a ship and trained while at sea. Not long after the Spanish-American War, the "U.S. Navy leaders noticed a remarkable fact. Many of their best Sailors came from the great American Midwest," according to the Navy Training Command.[22] So the top brass decided to locate the training center on the southwestern shore of Lake Michigan in Illinois. But there was a hitch. Land cost about $1,000 per acre, which was a lot of money at the time. The navy wouldn't pay it, and the project stalled for several years.
>
> Finally, though, an unusual event took place. Under the leadership of U.S. Congressman George E. Foss of Illinois, a group of wealthy and patriotic businessmen in Chicago bought 172 acres of wilderness land on Lake Michigan at a cost of $100,000. In 1905, the group turned the acreage over to the navy for a price—$1.00—another remarkable fact! By the end of the year, construction was underway, and six years later, human hands with the aid of horses had built the original thirty-nine buildings of the Great Lakes Training Station.[23]

players, triggered by infrared technology, make "injured" dummies scream, moan and make faint breathing sounds. Thousands of gallons of water flood the ship's compartments. Flames jet from fire fighting areas. Floors shake to mimic the ship's movement.[24]

Once recruits successfully complete this realistic training test, they officially become sailors.

NOTES

1. Quoted in J. F. Leahy, *Honor, Courage, Commitment: Navy Boot Camp* (Annapolis, MD: Naval Institute Press, 2002), p. 19.

2. "Soldier Life—Basic Combat Training," n.d., www.goarmy .com/life/basic/index.jsp (accessed June 26, 2007).

3. "Soldier Life."

4. "Naval Term Origins," n.d., www.nautilus571.com/ naval_terms.htm (accessed June 23, 2007).

5. See marines.com/page/usmc.jsp?pageId=/page/SubSection-XML-Conversion.jsp?pageName=Recruit-Training&flashRedirect=true (accessed June 26, 2007).

6. "During the Navy Boot Camp," n.d., www.navy.com/about/ during/bootcamp (accessed June 26, 2007).

7. See U.S. Air Force Enlisted Basic Training, www.airforce .com/training/enlisted/index.php, and United States Coast Guard Cape May, www.uscg.mil/hq/capemay (accessed June 23, 2007).

8. John Dunipace, "Transcript: Corporal John Dunipace Letter, Co. I, 144th Ohio Volunteer Infantry," Center for Archival Collections, University Libraries at Bowling Green, Ohio, June 24, 1864, www.bgsu.edu/colleges/library/cac/transcripts/ms0484t9a.html (accessed June 23, 2007).

9. Ferris W. Myrice, "WWI Diary," Center for Archival Collections, University Libraries at Bowling Green, Ohio, 1918–1919, www.bgsu.edu/colleges/library/cac/transcripts/ mms1729.html (accessed June 23, 2007).

10. "Time Frame: Boot Camp thru Shipping over Continuous from April 1917," *In Their Own Words*, n.d., www.worldwar1 .com/dbc/ow_2.htm (accessed June 23, 2007).

11. Byron Armbruster, Letter, Center for Archival Collections, University Libraries at Bowling Green, Ohio, April 1942, www .bgsu.edu/colleges/library/cac/transcripts/ms0984t105.html#420401 (accessed June 23, 2007).

12. "The Personal Memoir of William L Sprague, Signalman Third Class, U.S. Coast Guard," April 2005, www.uscg.mil/history/ WEBORALHISTORY/WWII_William_Sprague_Memoir.html (accessed June 23, 2007).

13. Donna Ione Smith, USCGR World War II Coast Guard SPAR Veteran, Interview, U.S. Coast Guard Oral History Program, Victoria Miller, interviewer, September 28, 2005, www.uscg.mil/ history/WEBORALHISTORY/donna_ione_smith_wwii_oralhistory .html (accessed June 23, 2007).

14. J. D. Leipold, "TRADOC: Morphing Civilians into Soldiers," Army News Service, June 23, 2006, www4.army.mil/ news/article.php?story=9205 (accessed January 8, 2008).

15. Quoted in Leipold, "TRADOC."

16. Quoted in Fred W. Baker III, "The Newest Warriors: A Look at Basic Training through the Eyes of Recruits," TRADOC News Service, February 18, 2004, www.tradoc.army.mil/pao/training_ closeup/023704.htm (accessed June 23, 2007).

17. Baker, "Newest Warriors."

18. "Basic Training 101—Acronyms and Abbreviations and Terms Commonly Used in Basic Combat Training," Basic Combat Training, Fort Jackson, South Carolina, n.d., www.jackson.army.mil/ BCT/101.htm (accessed June 23, 2007).

19. Quoted in Fred W. Baker III, "Basic Combat Training Week 9: Soldiers, Finally," TRADOC News Service, April 16, 2004, www.tradoc.army.mil/pao/training_closeup/043204.htm (accessed June 23, 2007).

20. Quoted in J. F. Leahy, p. 19.

21. Leahy, pp. 38–41.

22. Rich Lara, NTC staff, "The Founding of Great Lakes," c. 2001, www.nsgreatlakes.navy.mil/history/index.html and www.nsgreatlakes.navy.mil/history/index2.html (accessed June 23, 2007).

23. Lara, "The Founding of Great Lakes."

24. Naval Service Training Command, "Battle Stations 21," n.d. www.nstc.navy.mil/battle_stations_21_New.htm (accessed January 7, 2008).

Choosing a
Military Career

In spite of arguments over recruitments and who should take up arms in wartime, thousands of teens choose to follow a long career in the armed forces, serving until they are eligible for retirement. Some teenagers aspire to be military officers. After high school graduation, Casey Czarzasty of Maryland reported that he wanted "to attend the United States Naval Academy in Annapolis, Maryland. I have decided to push myself to my limits—physically and mentally. This also means that I will be an officer in the United States Navy."[3]

Students may begin their path toward a military career by joining the Junior Reserve Officers' Training Corps (JROTC) while in high school. JROTC provides leadership training for students and inspires positive attitudes toward military service. However, JROTC programs do not produce military officers. At the college level, students may apply for the Reserve Officers' Training Corps (ROTC), which trains young adults to become officers in the U.S. Army, Marine Corps, Navy, and Air Force after they graduate. ROTC programs are offered at more than one thousand colleges and universities throughout the United States. As part of their college curriculum, students in these programs take classes in military science, participate in leadership training, and learn how to conduct missions as officers. There are also ROTC summer programs that provide additional training and a sample of military life, such as midshipmen cruises in Naval ROTC.

Another avenue to becoming an officer in the armed forces is through federal service academies of the Air Force, Army,

"I want to enroll in one of the academies or ROTC not because I need money for school but because I want to serve my great country."

—an anonymous Austin, Texas, high school student[1]

"I want to be an Air Force officer to have the privilege of serving my country and fulfilling my duty as an American citizen."

—Emma L. Rush, who entered the U.S. Air Force Academy in 2006[2]

Coast Guard, Merchant Marine, and Navy. The U.S. government operates these academies, and students wishing to attend must be nominated by a member of Congress, a congressional delegate, the vice president, or a career military officer. The U.S. Coast Guard Academy (USCGA) is the only one that does not require an appointment but accepts candidates based on a national academic competition, which includes a review of test scores and high school transcripts.

CAREER CHOICES

Nineteen-year-old Liesl Marelli was a student at Montclair State University in New Jersey when New York's World Trade Center was attacked by terrorists in 2001. She felt duty bound to do something for her country and decided to sign up in 2002 for the New Jersey National Guard, where she spent three years. She was deployed stateside for two years, and her duties included completing paperwork for injured or killed U.S. troops. In 2006, she was working for the Illinois National Guard in Springfield while also completing her university degree. During an NPR interview, she said, "I happen to love my full-time job working here, surprisingly enough. I figure, if you wake up loving what you do, why leave it?"[4] She is thinking about a career in the military.

What are the choices of careers? There are more than 140 varied occupations in the military, including accounting, aviation, combat operations, construction, engineering, graphic design, intelligence, legal professions, mechanics, medical technology, social work, vehicle driving, and warehouse work. Suppose a person wants to work in communications and electronics. In the U.S. Air Force, her or his job would include installing, modifying, maintaining, repairing, and overhauling airborne and ground TV equipment, data-processing equipment, cryptographic machine systems, teletypewriters, and various electronic test equipment. The U.S. Department of Defense provides public information on military careers on its website, Careersinthemilitary.com. For example, a variety of creative and artistic jobs in all branches of the military are described. As the Department of Defense's website notes,

> a photojournalist might capture images of a humanitarian-relief operation in a foreign country, an audiovisual technician might film an important news conference, a graphics designer might create graphics for a high-profile Pentagon presentation or design layouts for a military newspaper or magazine, or a musician might perform at a presidential inauguration or special celebration for foreign dignitaries.[5]

Perhaps an enlistee would like to be a dietician in the army, navy, or air force. After training, that person would be responsible for such tasks as setting policies for hospital food service operations, developing special diets for patients based on instructions from doctors, planning menus, and providing information on nutrition to the military community.

Profiles of military career people are also included on the Department of Defense's website. A few are summarized here:

- Michael Mead grew up in Michigan and after high school graduation enlisted in the marines. In his words: "For as long as I can remember, I had always wanted to be in the military."[6] After his initial training, he received overseas assignments in Japan, Guam, and Iraq. His platoon was ambushed in 2003 in Iraq, and he suffered shrapnel and burn wounds. After physical therapy and rehabilitation, he reenlisted with his unit and deployed again to Iraq. As he puts it: "I felt that I owed it to the friends I had lost to continue to do my part. On this tour, I helped Iraqis build their own defense. We taught them how to patrol and become tactically proficient. By the time we left, the Iraqis were able to conduct their own patrols and raids."[7]

- Mi Sou Hood hadn't planned to join the military after high school, but she notes her career army father "encouraged me to apply for a scholarship to help pay for my education." She followed her father's advice and earned a B.S. in math and biology. Hood did not complete the AFROTC program, so she enlisted in the air force for two years. She says, "Those two years of enlistment were very good for me and have made me a better officer today because I know what it's like to be an enlisted Airman."[8] During her enlistment, she also earned her associate degree in information management. Later, she received officer training and eventually "became an Officer in Charge (OIC) for Network Administration and Support. I was directly responsible for the oversight of help desk communications, network administration, web operations and configuration management."[9] In her view

> the career field of communications is very broad. It deals with telephones, computers, land mobile radios, Blackberries and almost any device involved in communication. Communications is an exciting field. It is constantly evolving with new technologies. I attend and also help sponsor technology expositions so that we can meet the growing communication needs of the Air Force.[10]

Nancy Tita tells about her army career, which has provided her with "the opportunity to travel, meet different people, learn the latest technologies, and just have fun. I joined the Army Reserves for training so I could do something different from my civilian job as a clerk." She volunteered for active duty and requested machinist training because of the challenge. After initial training, she says her "first assignment was at Fort Eustis [Virginia] where I worked in the maintenance company, helping make repairs to everything from radios to helicopters. I was able to learn my trade quickly and became familiar with some of the other occupations in the maintenance shop." She also gained expertise as a medical technician and served in Korea for a year. She reports that after returning to the United States, she "became a shop foreman in the services section of an armored division at Fort Knox [Kentucky]. In this position, I supervised a crew that repaired jeeps, tanks, and other armored equipment." Her most recent assignment at Aberdeen Proving Ground is "instructor and noncommissioned officer in charge of student control. In addition to teaching metalworking courses, I process students entering training and assign them to their various classes." Promoted to staff sergeant, she looks "forward to being one of the top-ranking females in the maintenance field. I like the challenge of being the only female in the unit."[11]

Dwayne Robinson "joined the Navy right after high school to travel and to learn a trade."[12] He discovered that he liked cooking and worked as a seaman apprentice in a mess hall and then in the galley of a ship before the navy sent him to cooking school. After his training, his "career really took off."[13] He won promotions and eventually achieved the rank of chief petty officer. He notes

> The most important day of my career was the day that I put on the hat, signifying that I had become a chef.
>
> A few years later, I was senior chef on the USS *New Orleans*. I managed a 35-person staff that fed 580 crew members and, at times, 1,800 Marines (nearly 7,000 meals a day). Aboard my last ship, the USS *Wadsworth*, I went on a 7-month cruise of the South Pacific, with stops in Hawaii, Guam, Korea, Hong Kong, the Philippines, Australia, New Zealand, and Samoa. I have spent the past several years as a food services supervisor on different ships and have done what I wanted to do—learn to cook and travel around the world.[14]

U.S. Army Warrant Officer Christopher J. Callaghan has opted for a military career. This photo was taken during a formation at Fort Bragg, site of American special forces. Photo courtesy of his parents, Dan and Anni Callaghan.

FINDING FISH (A FILM AND MEMOIR)

The 2002 film *Finding Fish* directed by Denzel Washington is based on the autobiography *Finding Fish: A Memoir* by Antwone Quenton Fisher with Mim Eichler Rivas. Fisher also wrote the screenplay and helped direct the movie, whose opening scene depicts a reunion with his family—people he never knew while growing up or during his early adulthood.

In the drama, Fisher's story involves his father's death—he was accidentally killed by a girlfriend. He is born to a single mother in jail who couldn't care for him and suffers years of abuse in a foster home of a storefront preacher and his cruel wife. He is eventually forced to live on the streets.

While a teenager, Fisher, played by Derek Luke, enlists in the navy to escape his harrowing life. But being a sailor at first does little to ease the rage he has suppressed because of his traumatic childhood, and he lashes out at his shipmates, sometimes violently. During his eleven years in the navy, a naval psychiatrist, played by Washington, helps Fisher face his past. Fisher also begins to nurture his talent as a poet and writer. The movie has been called a tear-jerker as well as inspiring and shows how Fisher overcomes adversity with not only the psychiatrist's support but also by his own perseverance.

AN OFFICER CAREER VIA MILITARY ACADEMIES

Almost everyone who is interested in the military has heard of or read about U.S. service academies. The U.S. Military Academy (West Point) is the oldest and most well known. Others are the U.S. Air Force Academy, the U.S. Naval Academy, the USCGA, and the U.S. Merchant Marine Academy. The latter is under the jurisdiction of the U.S. Department of Transportation. West Point, south of New York City on the Hudson River, was founded in 1802. The Naval Academy, founded in 1845, is in Annapolis, Maryland. New London, Connecticut, is the home of the USCGA, founded in 1876. And Kings Point, New York, was dedicated in 1943 as the site for the Merchant Marine Academy. Established in 1954, the Air Force Academy is in Colorado, north of Colorado Springs.

It is no simple matter to gain admission to an academy. A candidate must be at least seventeen years old, not more than twenty-three years old for West Point and the Naval and Air Force Academies (no more than twenty-two years old for the USCGA), unmarried, not pregnant, and not legally obligated to support children. Candidates also have to qualify academically, medically, and physically. If accepted, cadets, as students are called, must commit to up to five years of active duty in the armed forces plus several more years in the reserves. Each of the academies maintains a website with information about applications, scholarships, allotments, majors offered, and addresses and phone numbers of the academies.[15]

At the end of the school year in 2003, four teenagers from western Pennsylvania told a reporter for the *Pittsburgh Tribune-Review* how they felt about becoming cadets at military academies. Karisa Walker was accepted at the Air Force Academy and was very impressed with the campus. She predicted it would be "quite different" after she arrived there and found "somebody already looking forward to yelling at me."[16] To Christopher Marsh, appointed to the Naval Academy, it was "clear to me that the academy certainly doesn't allow you to be lazy. I'll be pushed both in mind and

WORDS FROM A COAST GUARD CADET

Caitlin Cunningham of Minnesota became a cadet at the USCGA in 2006, and near the end of her first year (April 2007), she assessed her experience as "the right choice" for her and "a growing experience."[17] Writing for an online USCGA journal, Cunningham offers advice for appointees facing Swab Summer, a seven-week traditional military indoctrination. She notes:

I had a lot of questions about the summer and how to prepare. It is difficult to put words to your life here. Physical experience is the only way to grow and learn.

For those appointees who are reading, my advice for the challenge ahead of you is to develop your inner self-confidence. You will probably be humbled when you come, because you will be working with many talented young people. I think the biggest piece of advice I can give is to give every task your all. If you work hard, it will be noticed. During the summer it helps if you blend in with the rest of your "company" (the group you are put with). Do your job adequately, and the summer will go smoothly for you. I have found that by focusing on what I can control, and not dwelling on what I cannot, I am a more positive person. Attitude is very important. When things are tough, the best way to make it through is to stay positive. Your career in the Coast Guard begins with yourself, and the coming year will help you grow.[18]

body, and I want to see how much more I can do and become."[19] Christopher Donohoe, also appointed to the Air Force Academy, notes that because he was in the ROTC during his first year in college, he thought he had "an idea of what's going to be expected," but he admitted that his college days of "fun" and freedom would be over.[20] David Flaherty's first impression of West Point, where he was appointed, was "perfection beyond belief." He was "anxious about getting started" and points out that he and other cadets would "have to walk on the grounds with our hands closed, [not] speak to upperclassmen, [and march in] formation for every meal."[21]

What happens after a cadet graduates from one of the academies? At West Point, a graduate receives a bachelor of science degree and is commissioned a second lieutenant in the U.S. Army. He or she must serve as an officer for at least five years. Graduates from the Air Force, Navy, Coast Guard, and Merchant Marine Academies also are awarded B.S. degrees and become commissioned officers.

NOTES

1. Nonmilitary Options for Youth, "Survey Responses, Westlake High School," October 20, 2005, www.progressiveaustin .org/nmofy/drupal//?q=node/86 (accessed June 16, 2007).

2. Senator John Cornyn, "Cornyn: Hope for Our Continuing Strength," Special to the Bryan-College Station *Eagle*, May 28, 2006, www.theeagle.com/stories/052806/opinions_ 20060528024.php (accessed June 23, 2007).

3. "In Their Own Words: Future Plans," *eJournal USA* (electronic journal of the U.S. State Department), July 2005, usinfo.state.gov/journals/itsv/0705/ijse/future.htm (accessed June 24, 2007).

4. David Schaper, "Suburban Teen Trades in Gucci for Army Green," NPR's *Day to Day*, September 12, 2006, www.npr.org/ templates/story/story.php?storyId=6056806 (accessed June 19, 2007).

5. *Careers in the Military*, "Arts, Communications, Media, and Design," n.d., careersinthemilitary.com/index.cfm?fuseaction= main.jobfamily (accessed November 8, 2007).

6. Michael Mead profile, *Careers in the Military*, n.d., www.careersinthemilitary.com/index.cfm?fuseaction=main .profiledetail&profile_id=25 (accessed January 7, 2008).

7. Mead profile, *Careers in the Military*.

8. Mi Sou Hood profile, *Careers in the Military*, n.d., www.careersinthemilitary.com/index.cfm?fuseaction=main .profiledetail&profile_id=28 (accessed June 20, 2007).

9. Hood profile, *Careers in the Military*.

10. Hood profile, *Careers in the Military*.

11. Nancy Tita profile, *Careers in the Military*, n.d., www.careersinthemilitary.com/index.cfm?fuseaction=main .profiledetail&profile_id=43 (accessed June 20, 2007).

12. Dwayne Robinson profile, *Careers in the Military*, n.d., www.careersinthemilitary.com/index.cfm?fuseaction=main .profiledetail&profile_id=30 (accessed June 20, 2007).

13. Robinson profile, *Careers in the Military*.

14. Robinson profile, *Careers in the Military*.

15. See U.S. Military Academy, www.usma.edu; U.S. Air Force Academy, www.usafa.af.mil; U.S. Naval Academy, www.nadn.navy.mil; U.S. Coast Guard Academy, www.cga.edu; U.S. Merchant Marine Academy, www.usmma.edu (accessed June 21, 2007).

16. Quoted in Gerard DeFlitch, "Local Teens Set Sights on Military Academies," *Pittsburgh Tribune-Review*, May 4, 2003, www.pittsburghlive.com/x/pittsburghtrib/s_132708.html (accessed June 21, 2007).

17. Caitlin Cunningham, "Cadet Life," *Cadet Journals*, April 2007, www.cga.edu/journal.aspx?id=5331## (accessed June 21, 2007).

18. Cunningham, "Cadet Life."

19. Quoted in DeFlitch, "Local Teens Set Sights on Military Academies."

20. Quoted in DeFlitch, "Local Teens Set Sights on Military Academies."

21. Quoted in DeFlitch, "Local Teens Set Sights on Military Academies."

Color Barriers in the Military

Throughout American history, the armed services have included people of diverse races and ethnic backgrounds. But that does not mean the U.S. military has been tolerant of all Americans who have chosen or been drafted to serve and fight in U.S. wars. Discrimination in the military has been common from the American Revolutionary War to the present day, although prejudicial treatment of minority group personnel has decreased dramatically over the years.

BLACKS IN THE REVOLUTION

Black men and women have fought in every U.S. war. Free blacks and slaves fought with the rebels against the British during the American Revolution, but they were not necessarily welcomed. In fact, many white slave owners, including General George Washington, feared that armed blacks would revolt. Washington ordered recruiters not to allow blacks in the army, and the Continental army "agreed, unanimously, to reject all slaves, and by a great majority, to reject negroes altogether."[2] In addition, the Continental Congress asked the question "Ought not Negroes be excluded from the new enlistment, especially such as are slaves?" The response: "Agreed. That they be rejected altogether."[3]

On the other side, the British were eager to recruit blacks and offered them their freedom if they would fight for England. That kind of enticement prompted the Continental Congress to reverse its decision to exclude blacks from

"Indian people fought for this country and we had good reason because this is our country. But I wasn't granted [state] citizenship until after the war. . . . It was all backward. They should have given me [Mississippi] citizenship before I went into the Army."

—Frank Henry, a member of the Mississippi Band of Choctaw Indians who was seventeen years old when he joined the army during World War II[1]

JAMES FORTEN, A TEEN PRIVATEER

James Forten, a black teenager who was born free in Philadelphia, enlisted at the age of fourteen as a powder boy on the privateer, the *Royal Louis*. He carried gun powder for the cannons as well as helped hoist sails, swab decks, and many other jobs aboard. The ship engaged in a victorious battle with the British, but when it sailed again, the *Royal Louis* fell to the British, and the crew became prisoners of war.

Forten feared the worst. Usually the British sent black prisoners to the West Indies, where they were sold into slavery, but according to one account, "his destiny, by a kind Providence, was otherwise."[4] Forten was placed onboard the British ship *Amphyon*. The ship's Captain Beasly decided that the teenager would make a good companion for his young son, who was making his first voyage. As the story goes,

> during one of those dull and monotonous periods which frequently occur on ship-board, young Beasly and Forten were engaged in a game at marbles, when, with signal dexterity and skill, the marbles were upon every trial successively displaced by the unerring hand of Forten. This excited the surprise and admiration of his young companion, who, hastening to his father, called his attention to it.[5]

Young Beasly so admired Forten that he persuaded his father to take Forten to England where he would be educated and live a luxurious life, but Forten refused. He reportedly told the captain, "I am here a prisoner for the liberties of my country; *I never*, never, *shall prove a traitor to her interests*!"[6]

Forten was sent to a British prison barge called the *Jersey* moored off New York. It was a filthy, airless ship crammed with sick and dying prisoners. Hundreds died while imprisoned, although Forten and others survived and were released in a prisoner exchange. After much hardship, Forten went on to become a successful businessman and a leader of the African American community in Philadelphia.

military service. The Continental army desperately needed troops, so slaves were promised their freedom and free blacks received cash upon enlistment. In some cases, slaves served as substitutes for their white owners. About five thousand blacks fought on the revolutionary side, while double that number signed on with the British.

In contrast to the army, the Continental navy recruited seamen of any color to serve on its ships. Because the navy had only thirty-one ships, Congress authorized private merchant vessels to be equipped as warships to fight the British at sea.

AFRICAN AMERICANS IN OTHER WARS

African Americans served in other wars, such as the War of 1812, which again pitted Americans against the British. It also brought African Americans into armed conflict with Native Americans, who aligned themselves with the British. Tribal groups hoped that by fighting on the side of the British they could force out settlers who were taking their land and destroying their way of life. After the War of 1812 ended in late 1814, discrimination against people of color in the military once more became common practice. The federal government and various states banned African Americans and Native Americans from serving in the U.S. Army, Marine Corps, or state militias. Racism played a major role and so did the fact that the nation was at peace and the armed forces had been reduced.

The Civil War changed the military makeup once more. Both the North and the South debated whether to allow African Americans and Native Americans to bear arms. During the first year of the war, blacks were not accepted in the Union army, but by the end of 1862, they were fighting for the Yankees and served with distinction. The Confederates forced some slaves to serve, but African Americans were not necessarily loyal. In one instance, slaves were able to take over a Rebel (or Confederate) gunboat anchored in Charleston

BUFFALO SOLDIERS

At the end of the Civil War in 1866, the U.S. Army formed the first regular African American cavalry and infantry regiments, which combined in 1869 to form the Twenty-fourth and Twenty-fifth Infantry Units. They became known collectively as Buffalo Soldiers and were so admired that some black teenagers exaggerated their age a bit to join the units. Mark Matthews, for example, became a Buffalo Soldier when he was sixteen years old. He died at the age of 111 in 2005 and was buried at Arlington Cemetery.

A unique Buffalo Soldier was Cathay Williams, who enlisted in the army as William Cathay. Women had disguised themselves as men and had fought in the Revolutionary and Civil Wars, but Williams is the only documented female to have served among the Buffalo Soldiers. When she enlisted, she said she was twenty-two years old, but she might have been as young as sixteen. Even though U.S. Army regulations forbade the enlistment of women, only a cursory medical examination was required, so Williams was accepted as William Cathay and traveled throughout the West with her unit. After less than two years of service, Cathay reported that she was ill, which apparently prompted a thorough physical, revealing her secret. She was honorably discharged in 1868.

No one is certain how the Buffalo Soldiers got their name. Some historians say tribal warriors nicknamed the regiments Buffalo Soldiers because they fought as fiercely as the buffalo, and African Americans considered the name an honorary title. But during the 1990s, many Native Americans disagreed, and some members of the American Indian Movement (AIM) declared that Plains Indians used the term *Buffalo Soldier* disparagingly to indicate the soldiers with dark skin who helped kill their people. AIM members protested when the U.S. Postal Service issued a stamp in 1994 honoring Buffalo Soldiers, and they demonstrated at museums and other exhibits on Buffalo Soldier history.

The original Buffalo Soldiers were stationed mainly in Kansas, Texas, and New Mexico, where they had to face the prejudice of many white settlers and army officials. Nevertheless, they fought against Native Americans on a western frontier that extended from Montana and the Dakotas to Texas, New Mexico, and Arizona in the Southwest. They also were in armed conflicts against Mexican revolutionaries, outlaws, and cattle rustlers. They protected stagecoaches and crews building railroads, and they helped string telegraph lines, build outposts on the frontier, and map areas of the Southwest. Buffalo Soldiers also took part in combat during the Spanish-American War in Cuba in 1898.

harbor. With their families aboard, the slave crew sailed away
and turned the ship over to the Union.

· Between the Civil War and World War I, racism was a
major factor in the increasing discriminatory practices to
which black troops were subjected, such as segregated
substandard housing, faulty equipment, and inadequate food
supplies. Racism followed African American soldiers who
were sent to fight in Europe during World War I. Two African
American secretaries for the YMCA, Addie W. Hunton and
Kathryn M. Johnson, were assigned to canteens in France.
The canteens were actually temporary buildings—huts or
tents—for servicemen and housed a dispensary or were used
for religious services, movies, concerts, and recreational
activities. The YMCA attempted to achieve integration at the
time, but not all YMCA workers lived up to the Christian
ideals of the organization. Hunton and Johnson recorded the
type of segregation and discrimination that black soldiers
faced in their published account *Two Colored Women with
the American Expeditionary Forces*. They note that YMCA
officials in Paris were "considerate and courteous to its
colored constituency," but "there is no doubt that the attitude
of many of the white [YMCA] secretaries in the field was to
be deplored. They came from all parts of the United States,
North, South, East and West, and brought their native
prejudices with them."[7] Hunton and Johnson point out "our
soldiers often told us of signs on Y.M.C.A. huts which read,
'No Negroes Allowed'; and sometimes other signs would
designate the hours when colored men could be served . . . but
always, when the matter was brought to the attention of Mr.
W. S. Wallace, the regional secretary, he would immediately
see that they were removed."[8] They describe other incidents,
such as

> One secretary had a colored band come to his hut to
> entertain his men. Several colored soldiers followed the band
> into the hut. The secretary got up and announced that no
> colored men would be admitted. The leader of the band, a
> white man, by the way, immediately informed his men that

they need not play; whereupon all departed and there was no entertainment. . . .

Quite a deal of unpleasantness was experienced on the boats coming home. One secretary in charge of a party sailing from Bordeaux attempted to put all the colored men in the steerage. They rebelled and left the ship; whereupon arrangements were made to give them the same accommodations as the others.

On another boat there were nineteen colored welfare workers; all the women were placed on a floor below the white women, and the entire colored party was placed in an obscure, poorly ventilated section of the dining-room, entirely separated from the other workers by a long table of Dutch civilians. The writer immediately protested; the reply was made that southern white workers on board the ship would be insulted if the colored workers ate in the same section of the dining-room with them, and, at any rate, the colored people need not expect any such treatment as had been given them by the French.[9]

It was not until World War II that the U.S. military brought more African Americans into its ranks, although blacks still served in segregated units. For the first time, the U.S. Marine Corps dropped its ban on black enlistees, and around 17,000 African Americans became "Leathernecks," a term derived from the leather collar of the uniform Marines once wore. In the U.S. Navy, blacks were not excluded, but they could serve only as cooks or stewards.

Official photograph of twenty Tuskegee Airmen posing in front of a plane, n.d. Photo courtesy U.S. Army Air Force Training Command.

Even though African Americans were brought into the armed forces, there was no quick turnaround in white attitudes. Mitchell Higginbotham, who was one of the first black military airmen of World War II, was twenty-four years old when he faced a court martial because he and other famed Tuskegee Airmen entered an all-white officers club at Freeman Field in Indiana. He recalled for a reporter, "It was a slap in the face. . . . it did a lot of psychological damage to all of us."[10] Higginbotham is one of only a few surviving Tuskegee Airmen who served from

TUSKEGEE AIRMEN

Before the U.S. involvement in World War II, many U.S. military officials were under the false and prejudicial assumption that African Americans were not physically or psychologically suited for combat, particularly flight training with the U.S. Army Air Corps, which later became the U.S. Army Air Force. But in 1941, President Franklin D. Roosevelt launched what was called the "Tuskegee Experiment." The military expected the experiment to fail, however men in the program proved them wrong.

The Army Air Corps founded a flight school in Alabama at the historically black Tuskegee Institute founded by Booker T. Washington. There, for the first time in the history of the U.S. Army Air Corps, African American men were trained as pilots, meteorologists, intelligence and engineering officers, flight surgeons, mechanics, control tower operators, and in many other skills that support an air force squadron. Under the command of Captain Benjamin O. Davis Jr., who became the first African American general of the U.S. Air Force, African American fighter pilots fought in aerial battles over North Africa, Sicily, and Europe, flying in 15,553 sorties and 1,578 missions. From June 1944 to April 1945, the airmen flew two hundred bomber escort missions over most of central and southern Europe without losing a single bomber to the enemy. To white American bomber crews, they were reverently known as "Black Redtail Angels" because of the bright red painted on the tail assemblies of their aircraft.

1941 to 1949; the airmen received a Congressional Gold Medal in 2007.

Countless books, movies, videos, TV documentaries, and other media have presented the long African American struggle for civil rights. For thousands of blacks, though, the military after desegregation became an avenue toward equality. As Debra Dickerson writes:

When I joined the Air Force in 1980, my eyes were not on the wild blue yonder. All I wanted was a steady job and an escape route out of the inner city. In north St. Louis, black kids like me—the daughter of former Southern sharecroppers—weren't raised to think big. I was a timid, aimless, underachieving 20-year-old who tried hard not to make eye contact.[11]

Dickerson explained that after twelve years she went on to earn a college degree and a masters, and she credits the military for not lowering standards in order to help women or people of color reach their potential: "The system zeroed in on strengths in me I was years from seeing in myself."[12]

INDIGENOUS SOLDIERS

Discrimination against indigenous people in the military somewhat mirrors the black experience. Native Americans and African Americans fought with and against each other from the American Revolution through the Civil War. For example, tribal members fought for both the Union and the Confederacy. Confederate armies actively recruited among the Choctaw, Chickasaw, Cherokee, Creek, and Seminole nations. There is no accurate figure for the number who joined Rebel forces, but an estimated 3,600 Native people, primarily Seminole, fought with the Yankees.

OFF THE BOOK SHELF

We Were There: Voices of African American Veterans, from World War II to the War in Iraq by Yvonne Latty is a compilation of profiles and experiences of blacks in the military along with photographs of participants by Ron Tarver. The words of these men and women, many of whom enlisted or were drafted when they were teenagers, present stories that usually "never get told."[13] As a Vietnam veteran puts it, "Whenever I turn on the television or see a movie about the war, you don't see the black perspective."[14] This book, however, provides that perspective and shows how "African Americans in the military set an example for our nation," as Brigadier General Vincent Brooks notes.[15]

DID YOU KNOW?

In 1917 when World War I was underway, Native Americans were subject to the draft, but the draft applied to citizens, and no one knew how many tribal people were citizens. Many were under the jurisdiction of their tribe or nation. Some Native women became citizens when they married white men. Others gained citizenship by serving in the armed forces or through special laws. Unlike immigrants from other countries, many Native Americans were barred from the naturalization process that led to citizenship. But after World War I, Congress passed the Indian Citizenship Act of 1924, granting citizenship to all Native people born in the United States.

During World War I, military officials frequently debated whether American Indians should be integrated into all-white units or kept in segregated units as had been the case in the past. Eventually an estimated ten thousand to twelve thousand Native soldiers served and were integrated into white regiments, however both the military and civilians still stereotyped Native troops; they were seen as members of a martial race with a fondness for war—warriors by nature, enthusiastic about fighting. They also were thought to have natural instincts for scouting and patrol duty, supernatural abilities to see and hear things that members of other ethnic groups could not. The stereotypical images of Native fighters prevailed through World War II and the armed conflicts in Korea, Vietnam, and the Persian Gulf. Native veterans frequently tell of being sent on some of the most dangerous missions because their commanding officers believed they had no fear of the enemy and that "rigors of combat hold no terrors" for them, as Secretary of Interior Harold Ickes declared in 1944.[16]

HONORABLE NATIVE TRADITION

When compared to other ethnic groups, Native Americans per capita have the highest record of military service. In Native culture, serving in the military is an honorable tradition, and those who serve are held in high esteem. Long before explorers came to the North American continent, indigenous people honored the warriors who protected their tribal members. As a Dakota/Lakota veteran explains, "It was always the warrior who was first in defending Mother Earth. It was his duty to be first. It is a part of traditional values, a part of protecting against any outside invasion that would endanger the people, our people and the land."[17]

For a Native warrior, military service is much more than patriotism—it is a way to develop inner strength, to gain physical, mental, and spiritual toughness. Being a warrior not only brings honor but also status within the community and pride in accomplishment. Tom Holm's book *Strong Hearts, Wounded Souls: Native American Veterans of the Vietnam War* shows that a majority of the veterans who were surveyed said that family tradition and tribal tradition were "very important" reasons for entering the service. One Vietnam veteran who was wounded and awarded the Silver Star states that he had "no particular loyalty to the United States" but instead was loyal "to my own people, my own tradition."[18] He points out, "We are pledged by a treaty to provide military assistance to the U.S. in times of war. I know that the U.S. has broken its part of the bargain with us, but we are more honorable than that. . . . we honor our commitments, always have and always will. . . . So, it was my obligation to do what I did, even though I didn't really want to."[19] While honoring treaty obligations was extremely important to this veteran, many others told Holm that "they had wanted to follow in the path of the old-time warriors: to gain respect from their own people for having done what young men have always done in times of conflict and by taking part in the traditional ceremonies of warfare reaffirming the tribal identity and special relationship with the spirit world."[20]

DISCRIMINATION AGAINST OTHER GROUPS

Along with African Americans and Native Americans, other minority groups have suffered discrimination in the military. For example, Asian Americans, including people of Japanese, Chinese, Filipino, and Korean ancestry, know what it feels like to be singled out for prejudicial treatment. Consider what happened to thousands of Filipino young adults—some teenagers and many in their twenties—who served in the U.S. armed forces during World War II. They enlisted or were drafted to fight against the Japanese who invaded the Philippines in 1941. The Philippines at the time was a commonwealth of the United States. To protect American interests there, the Philippine Commonwealth Constitution allowed the United States to draft Filipinos. Many in the Philippines considered this a patriotic duty—since childhood they had observed American holidays and many traditions and in school pledged allegiance to the U.S. flag. The United States had promised Philippine independence and U.S. citizenship to Filipinos once the war ended. But the Rescission Acts of 1946 declared that Filipino veterans would not be recognized as having been in "active service" because the Philippines was soon to become independent. As a result, Filipino World War II veterans were denied the benefits that U.S. veterans received, and they could not apply for citizenship. More than four decades later, "in 1990 Congress granted Filipino World War II veterans the same opportunity to naturalize offered to all other foreign nationals who served in the U.S. armed forces," according to a report in the *Washington Post.*[21]

In 2003, Congress passed the Veterans Benefits Act, which extended VA medical care to eight thousand Filipino veterans living in the United States. However, as of 2007, World War II veterans of the Commonwealth Army of the Philippines and Philippine resistance troops who served in the U.S. armed forces were still not entitled to full benefits due a U.S. veteran. In addition, Filipino veterans in the United States have been unable to unite with their family members because immigration laws require long waits—about sixteen years—for Filipinos to emigrate to the United States. Many Filipino veterans are in the United States because of health problems, and now in their eighties, they do not expect to live long enough to reunite with their families. Yet, there is some hope. Bills proposed by members of Congress in 2007 would allow children of Filipino World War II veterans to be exempt from the immigration waiting list.

World War II also resulted in clear discriminatory acts against Japanese Americans. An estimated 120,000 Japanese Americans on the West Coast, many of whom were citizens and veterans or families of military personnel, were forced out of their homes and businesses to "relocation centers"—actually concentration camps. These so-called enemy aliens were herded into hastily built barracks or converted horse stalls in remote areas of the California interior and Arizona, Arkansas, Colorado, Idaho, Montana, Utah, and Wyoming. Secretary of War Henry L. Stimson convinced President Franklin D. Roosevelt that American citizens of Japanese ancestry would turn against the United States even though there was no evidence of disloyalty. Such twisted reasoning was shared by many Americans at the time. Roosevelt signed Executive Order 9066 that required "all Japanese persons, both alien and non-alien" to be forcibly evacuated from the West Coast.

Japanese Americans, including Nisei—citizens whose parents were born in Japan—were not eligible for the draft, and those in the military were discharged or placed in segregated units that performed menial labor. In Hawaii, a U.S. territory at the time, Japanese Americans were not interred, but Nisei were not accepted in the National Guard. Frank Sogi, who was a young man at the time, recalled "I served in Hawai'i Territorial Guard for about a month or two,

and we were called in and they said that . . . we were
considered 'enemy aliens.' We were Japanese Americans
nevertheless, and they said we were enemy aliens and that's
why we were discharged from the territorial guard."[22]

In 1943, President Roosevelt declared that "Americanism
is not, and never was, a matter of race or ancestry," and the
War Department announced that a segregated Japanese
American combat unit would be formed. The unit became the
442nd Regimental Combat Team—legendary soldiers who
battled in Europe. In spite of losing their freedom and civil
rights, more than twelve hundred Americans of Japanese
ancestry in the concentration camps enlisted in the army,
while about ten thousand Nisei in Hawaii volunteered.

Among the Nisei in Hawaii was Daniel Inouye, who later
became a U.S. senator. Inouye was seventeen years old when
the Japanese hit Pearl Harbor, and he was part of a first-aid
litter team to assist American casualties in the Pacific war. In
1943, he enlisted in the 442nd Regimental Combat Team and
went to the mainland for basic training. He was appalled
when the bus he was on with other recruits stopped at a camp
where he saw

> row after row of barracks. . . . High barbed wire fences and
> . . . machine gun towers all around the camp with men there
> with machine guns. And greeting us at the camp, at the gate,
> were men in uniform with rifles and bayonets. We are in
> uniform and I thought, "What in the world is happening?"
> . . . When we arrived, we were all singing and playing
> ukuleles and having a great time, and when we left, it was
> absolute silence. . . . No one talked. And I can imagine what
> was going through their minds, and I think almost all of us
> must have asked ourselves—would we have volunteered [had
> we known about the camps]?[23]

In 1943, the U.S. government reversed its position on
conscription and subjected Nisei to the draft. But dozens of
Japanese Americans in concentration camps resisted. Tak
Hoshizaki was one of them. He was attending Belmont High
School in Los Angeles when he and his family were forced

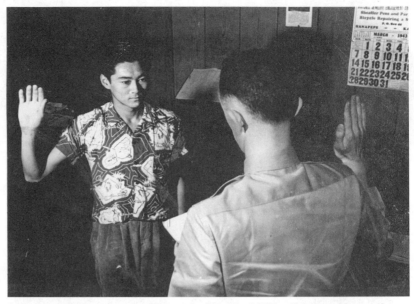

A Japanese American enlistee during World War II takes the oath.
U.S. Library of Congress photo.

into a detention camp in Wyoming. According to a PBS special, "Hoshizaki graduated high school inside camp. A half-year later he refused induction."[24] He and dozens of other young men were accused of violating the Selective Service Act. They were convicted and imprisoned. Two years later, an appeals court overturned their conviction, and in July 1946, they were released. President Truman pardoned all the draft resisters in December 1947.[25]

In 1948, Truman issued Executive Order 9981, which declared "there shall be equality of treatment and opportunity for all persons in the armed services without regard to race, color, religion or national origin. This policy shall be put into effect as rapidly as possible."[26] Truman's order certainly was a first step in reducing color barriers in the armed forces, but his policy did not take effect with any great speed. Prejudicial attitudes and segregation of troops continued during the Korean War in 1950. For example, African American troops were trained at a segregated facility at Fort Dix, New Jersey.

The secretary of defense abolished all segregated units in the armed forces in 1954. However, during the Vietnam War in the 1960s, racial tensions were high in many parts of the United States and also in the military. Discrimination against minorities and violent racial confrontations were common. As a result, in 1971 the Department of Defense established a Defense Race Relations Institute, later renamed the Defense Equal Opportunity Management Institute, which helped improve race relations through training programs. By the 1990s, the military had become one of the most integrated institutions in the nation, yet some members of the armed forces still face controversy over their roles in the military because of their gender, sexual orientation, or sometimes religious affiliation.

NOTES

1. Quoted in Rudi Williams, "Indians Fight America's Wars Because 'This Is Our Country, Too,'" American Forces Information Service, U.S. Department of Defense, November 21, 2002, www.defenselink.mil/news/Nov2002/n11212002_200211217.html (accessed June 17, 2007).

2. Leslie H. Fishel Jr. and Benjamin Quarles, *The Negro American: A Documentary History* (Glenview, IL: Scott, Foresman, 1967), p. 49.

3. Quoted in Fishel and Quarles, *Negro American*, p. 49.

4. William Nell Cooper, *The Colored Patriots of the American Revolution, With Sketches of Several Distinguished Colored Persons: To Which Is Added a Brief Survey of the Condition and Prospects of Colored Americans* (Boston: Robert F. Wallcut, 1855), p. 168; Electronic Edition, *Documenting the American South*, 1999, University Library, The University of North Carolina at Chapel Hill, docsouth.unc.edu/neh/nell/nell.html (accessed June 23, 2007).

5. Cooper, *Colored Patriots of the American Revolution*, p. 168.

6. Cooper, *Colored Patriots of the American Revolution*, p. 168.

7. Addie W. Hunton and Kathryn M. Johnson, *Two Colored Women with the American Expeditionary Forces* (Brooklyn, NY: Brooklyn Eagle Press, c. 1920), p. 26.

8. Hunton and Johnson, *Two Colored Women*, p. 26.

9. Hunton and Johnson, *Two Colored Women*, pp. 28–29.

10. Craig Smith, "Region's Tuskegee Airmen to be Honored," *Pittsburgh Tribune-Review,* March 26, 2007, www.pittsburghlive

.com/x/pittsburghtrib/news/cityregion/s_499576.html (accessed June 23, 2007).

11. Debra Dickerson, "The Martial Melting Pot: How the Military Encourages and Promotes Blacks without Lowering Its Standards," *U.S. News and World Report*, December 23, 1996, p. 32.

12. Dickerson, "Martial Melting Pot," p. 32.

13. Quoted in Yvonne Latty with photographs by Ron Tarver, *We Were There: Voices of African American Veterans, from World War II to the War in Iraq* (New York: Amistad/HarperCollins, 2004), p. 137.

14. Quoted in Latty, *We Were There*, p. 137.

15. Quoted in Latty, *We Were There*, p. 180.

16. Harold Ickes, "Indians Have a Name for Hitler," *Collier's*, January 15, 1944, p. 58.

17. Quoted in "Native American Veterans," U.S. Department of Housing and Urban Development, Homes and Communities, January 1, 2007, www.hud.gov/local/shared/working/r10/nwonap/veterans.cfm?STATE=wa (accessed June 23, 2007).

18. Quoted in Tom Holm, *Strong Hearts, Wounded Souls: Native American Veterans of the Vietnam War* (Austin: University of Texas Press, 1996), p. 118.

19. Quoted in Holm, *Strong Hearts*, p. 118.

20. Holm, *Strong Hearts*, p. 119.

21. N. C. Aizenman, "Hope for Amends to Filipino Immigrants," *Washington Post*, March 4, 2007, p. A6.

22. Japanese American National Museum, video interview, May 29, 2006, www.discovernikkei.org/en/people/clip.php?profileid=66&row=1 (accessed June 23, 2007).

23. Discover Nikkei, "Why Japanese Americans Volunteered for Service during WWII," November 7, 2006, www.discovernikkei.org/forum/node/1410 (accessed June 23, 2007).

24. PBS, *Conscience and the Constitution*, 2000 www.pbs.org/itvs/conscience/the_story/characters/hoshizaki_tak.html (accessed June 23, 2007).

25. PBS, *Conscience and the Constitution*.

26. President Harry Truman, Executive Order 9981, July 26, 1948, www.trumanlibrary.org/9981a.htm (accessed June 23, 2007).

7 "Equality of Treatment" for All?

The answer to that question would be a resounding "*no.*"
Females, who have served in some role in every U.S. war, have
not received equal treatment in the military over the years,
even though they are now recruited routinely for the U.S.
Army, Navy, Marine Corps, Air Force, and Coast Guard.
Gays and lesbians in the military are treated in what many
Americans consider a discriminatory manner. And some
military personnel who belong to non-Christian religious
groups say they regularly are subjected to prejudicial actions.

"I'm disappointed. I hope some day things will be different."

—Eighteen-year-old
Shane Bagwell, who
was denied enlistment
in the military because
he refused to hide his
homosexuality[1]

MILITARY WOMEN

About 175,000 to 200,000 women have served in the active
U.S. military since the beginning years of the twenty-first
century. About 70,000 women were in the army in 2005.[2]
However, being a female in the military is certainly not a new
phenomenon—as stated, women have served in every war,
primarily as nurses. Sometimes they were disguised as men or
were the wives of soldiers and fought alongside them in
Revolutionary and Civil War battles.

Although not well known, hundreds of women were
included in the U.S. Army Signal Corps during World War I,
but they were not considered equal to males. They were
telephone operators who at the time were called "Hello
Girls." They were supposed to meet certain criteria: be
bilingual (French/English), a minimum of twenty-five years
old, single, and have a college degree. They would serve

LEGENDARY DEBORAH SAMSON

No women were allowed to be soldiers in the Revolutionary War, but Deborah Samson was one of the first to defy that ban. She was born in 1760 and was part of a large family in Massachusetts. When her father deserted the family, her mother could not take care of all the children, so Deborah went to live with friends and relatives. At the age of ten, she was indentured to a farmer and worked at farm chores, growing muscular and tall. Although she had no formal schooling, she was able to get an education by having the farmer's sons review their school studies with her. She learned enough to become a schoolteacher at age eighteen, but with the last battles of the Revolutionary War underway, she wanted to join the fight. She made herself a man's suit and according to the legend walked thirty miles to enlist as Robert Shirtliffe.

She served for several years and fought in battles to protect the Hudson (River) Highlands. She was wounded twice. The first time, a saber cut her head, and she dressed the wound herself. Her second wound came from a musket ball that hit her in the thigh. She again tried to treat herself, but the wound became infected. She lost consciousness and was hospitalized. That ended her deception, but Robert Shirtliffe/Deborah Samson received an honorable discharge in 1783.

behind the lines in France and England to operate switchboards and connect generals with soldiers in the trenches.

More than seven thousand women applied for the Signal Corps. Many did not meet the criteria, and only 450 were selected for service. Because operators were sorely needed, rules were waived in some cases, and on occasion, teenagers from age sixteen to nineteen were chosen. According to an official Fort Gordon (Georgia) Army website for the Signal Corps Museum, "The women received military and Signal Corps training . . . in basic military radio procedures."[3] They wore regulation uniforms with Signal Corps patches; were issued dog tags, gas masks, and steel helmets; and were

World War I Army Signal Corps "Hello Girls." Photo courtesy U.S. Army.

required to follow all army regulations. The first operators were sent to Europe in the spring of 1918, and some served at the front, taking enemy fire.

After the armistice in 1919, the Hello Girls requested honorable discharges and World War I medals, but they were denied. They were told they were not eligible for veteran's status because all army regulations referred to males only. The operators were considered civilians working for the army. Over several decades, congressional bills were introduced to change the regulations, but the proposed law was always buried in committee; "it took one of the operators, Mearle Eagan Anderson, over fifty years of persistence to secure legislation to award the operators veteran's status. In 1978, President Jimmy Carter signed the bill giving the women their deserved recognition."[4]

Women were not recognized formally as part of the military until the 1940s, when the Women's Army Auxiliary Corps (WAAC)—which became the Women's Army Corp (WAC)—and Women Appointed for Volunteer Emergency Service (WAVES) were founded. Women in the WAC were postal workers, clerks, typists, and medical technicians; they repaired armor and military trucks, operated teletype machines, and worked in chemical laboratories.

By the 1960s and 1970s, women were serving alongside men in the Vietnam War, but they were not allowed on the front

These four members of the Women Air Force Service Pilots (WASP), a civilian group, were trained during World War II to ferry aircraft from factories to military bases, thus freeing male pilots for combat duty. Photo courtesy U.S. Air Force.

Female marines march during a parade at Camp Foster, Okinawa, Japan, around the time of the Korean War. The number of women on active duty during the Korean War reached peak strength at 2,787. Photo courtesy U.S. Marine Corps.

lines. In the Persian Gulf wars since then, women have been banned from combat. Army regulations bar women from support units that are embedded with combat troops. For example, women who are medics cannot go to the front lines with an infantry unit.

Nevertheless they have been attacked in bunkers and in convoys carrying supplies, and they have died. More women have been killed in Iraq than in any other war. To name and honor just a few: twenty-three-year-old Pfc. Lori Ann Piestewa, a member of the Hopi Nation of Tuba City, Arizona, was the first Native American woman ever to die in combat on foreign soil. She was killed in action in 2003 after her convoy was ambushed in Iraq. Twenty-one-year-old Pfc. Analaura Esparza Gutierrez of Houston, Texas, was killed in Tikrit. She was in a convoy that was hit by rocket-propelled grenades. Nineteen-year-old Pfc. Rachel Bosveld of Waupun,

Wisconsin, was killed during a mortar attack in Baghdad. Eighteen-year-old Pfc. Leslie D. Jackson of Richmond, Virginia, died in Baghdad when her military vehicle hit an improvised explosive device. Hundreds of other young adults between the ages of 18 and 22 are included in the nearly 4,000 Americans who have died in the Iraq War (as reported by the Associated Press on January 3, 2008). In spite of this, many women in the armed forces say they should not be banned from combat units. They reason that due to the guerrilla nature of the war, they often are in the direct line of fire anyway. That argument has not had any great impact, however, and no one expects the issue of women in combat to be resolved decisively any time soon.

SEXUAL HARASSMENT

Sexual harassment first gained widespread public attention after passage of the Civil Rights Act of 1964—women were able to file lawsuits against employers and others who discriminated against them because of gender. Such discrimination includes sexual harassment, which basically is unwanted and unwelcome sexual behavior. And it is illegal.

Sexual harassment in the military did not get widespread attention until a case that involved navy and marine officers was publicized following two reports by the Department of Defense (DoD). The incident took place during a 1991 Las Vegas convention of naval aircraft-carrier fighter pilots, an annual event called Tailhook, named for the hook on the aircraft that snags and stops jets as they land on carriers. More than five thousand navy and marine officers attended the weekend convention, which traditionally had been organized to bring retired and active-duty officers together for professional seminars, golf outings, and evening parties. Only about 4 percent of the officers were women, among them helicopter pilot Lt. Paula Coughlin, who was an aide to a rear admiral at the time. Daughter of a career naval aviator, she had been taught that naval officers were honorable and heroic people, but all that changed in Las Vegas.

She attended a formal dinner at the convention and later went to a hospitality suite where officers had gathered. When she walked down a hall toward the suite, about two dozen pilots were lined along the walls. One yelled "admiral's aide!" and Coughlin was grabbed by the buttocks so forcefully that she was lifted off the floor. She angrily confronted the pilot who had assaulted her, but others joined in the attack, grabbing her breasts and reaching under her skirt to pull at her underpants. She yelled for help, but no one came to her aid. She was finally able to kick, claw, and bite her way free.

Along with Coughlin, dozens of other female guests were assaulted. They reported the incidents to navy officials, who investigated and released a report that identified only two suspects, which to some congressional members and much of the public indicated a cover-up. Coughlin's mother, a career officer's wife, urged her daughter to speak to the press. The news stories and public scandal that followed prompted the Office of the Inspector General of the DoD to issue a report citing a failure of leadership and creating an atmosphere that allowed at least ninety indecent assaults to occur.

The report also included graphic descriptions and photographs documenting the lewd, drunken behavior of male officers. Because of the scandal, the secretary of the navy was forced to resign, as were three admirals, and some officers were denied promotions. The disciplinary actions did little, however, to stop the sexual harassment of and retaliation against Paula Coughlin. She decided she was no longer able to serve effectively and submitted her letter of resignation to the secretary of the navy in 1994.

Since Tailhook, other cases of sexual harassment and assault have made news. For example, in 1999, incidents of rape, sexual assault, and sexual harassment occurred at the army's Aberdeen (Maryland) Proving Grounds, and several drill sergeants were convicted of rape or sexual harassment and were court-martialed. A *Washington Post* story notes that in 2005 "more than half the women studying at the Naval, Air Force and Army academies reported experiencing some form of sexual harassment on campus." The article explains that the survey of female cadets was "conducted largely in response to allegations of widespread sexual harassment and assault at the [Colorado] Air Force Academy in 2003."[5]

The DoD took steps in 2004 to eliminate instances of sexual assault by establishing Sexual Assault Prevention and Response Programs throughout the armed forces. The army, for example, now has a "comprehensive policy that centers on awareness and prevention, training and education, victim advocacy, response, reporting, and accountability. Army policy promotes sensitive care and confidential reporting for victims of sexual assault and accountability for those who commit these crimes."[6]

The U.S. *Air Force News* reports that DoD officials have made an "effort to create a 'climate of confidence'" by giving victims of sexual assault "an option of restricted or unrestricted reporting. When filing a restricted report, victims could receive medical care and counseling for assaults without alerting their chain of command or triggering an investigation." As a result, there has been a "65 percent increase in reporting." According to the *News*, there were 756 restricted reports in 2006, but after medical treatment and counseling, 86 of the victims "changed their reports to unrestricted status, allowing the pursuit of those who acted against them."[7]

In spite of the reforms, some women who have tried to report sexual harassment and assault have not received help. Women who turn in perpetrators frequently are without advocates, according to Helen Benedict, who is writing a nonfiction book, *Women at War: Combat and Conscience in Iraq*. Benedict interviewed numerous Iraq veterans for her book. One was twenty-one-year-old Mickiela Montoya. She was with the National Guard in Iraq in 2005. Montoya told the author that she always carried a knife with her to ward off attacks: "The knife wasn't for the Iraqis. It was for the guys on my own side."[8]

"DON'T ASK, DON'T TELL"

Jarrett Lucas, twenty; Shane Bagwell, eighteen; and Marissa Cotroneo, nineteen—all from Pennsylvania—tried to enlist in

MILITARY DEFINITION OF SEXUAL HARASSMENT

In the U.S. military, sexual harassment is defined as a "form of gender discrimination that involves unwelcome sexual advances, requests for sexual favors, and other verbal or physical conduct of a sexual nature."[9] Two types of sexual harassment are defined:

- *Quid pro quo* sexual harassment refers to conditions placed on a person's career or terms of employment in return for sexual favors. It involves threats of adverse actions if the victim does not submit or promises of favorable actions if the person does submit.
- *Hostile environment* sexual harassment occurs when a person is subjected to offensive, unwanted, and unsolicited comments and behavior of a sexual nature that interferes with that person's work performance or creates an intimidating, hostile, or offensive working environment.

In addition, the military makes clear the difference between sexual harassment and sexual assault, a crime punishable under the Uniform Code of Military Justice. Sexual assault "can occur without regard to gender or spousal relationship or age of victim."[10] It includes rape, forcible sodomy, and indecent assault.

the U.S. military in 2006, but they were all denied because they refused to hide their homosexuality. In other words, they did not comply with the military policy of "Don't Ask, Don't Tell." One recruiter told them to lie about their sexual orientation if they were serious about enlisting. "I would love to serve," said Cotroneo; "we're very hurt that our country is rejecting us."[11]

Before the "Don't Ask, Don't Tell" policy went into effect, homosexuals were banned from the military, and those in the armed forces discovered to be gay were discharged. Throughout World War II and the decades between 1950 and 1980, homosexuality was called a "psychiatric disorder"

or a "moral defect," and homosexuals were considered untrustworthy because they might be subject to blackmail or were thought to be too effeminate to be good soldiers. Yet homosexuals have served quietly and heroically in the armed forces for decades.

In 1993, the ban against gays and lesbians in the military was lifted as long as the "Don't Ask, Don't Tell" policy was followed. One defender insists that the policy creates a "neutral environment, without judgments of morality" and draws a "line between [soldiers'] own sexual identity and the need to actively demonstrate for it."[12] Gay and lesbian groups have opposed it, calling it legalized discrimination. They and their supporters have urged congressional members to repeal the policy that has resulted in thousands of discharges plus nearly $200 million to recruit and train replacements. Many of the soldiers discharged had important and needed skills, such as data processing; voice interpretation; and knowledge of Arabic, Farsi, and Korean languages.

RELIGIOUS INTOLERANCE IN THE MILITARY

Like citizens across the United States, military personnel are followers of diverse religious beliefs, and religious denominations ordain chaplains to serve the armed forces. Chaplains are military officers and provide worship services—which are voluntary—and religious ceremonies, such as baptisms, confirmations, marriages, and last rites. Other military personnel in the chaplaincy provide services. For example, Michael Kowalski, a chaplain assistant, explained that he "supported the Jewish chapel program . . . set up the field chapel tent, organized field services, and provided moral support to . . . individual soldiers."[13]

Chaplains, whatever their faith, are expected to respect religious pluralism and provide for the free exercise of religion by all military personnel and their family members, but that has not been the case in some instances. In 2005, for example, a team of U.S. Air Force officials reported on its investigation of the Air Force Academy and interviews with cadets who are primarily in the eighteen-to-twenty-two age range. The team found inappropriate proselytizing by some evangelical Christian cadets and officers at the academy. Some non-Christian cadets told the team that there was an "overtly Christian environment at USAFA," such as predominantly Christian prayer before mandatory events, which "all cadets are required to endure regardless of personal religious beliefs."[14] Complaints from Jewish cadets, according to the report, included "problems with religious tolerance among fellow cadets, some faculty, some leadership, and several athletic department coaches." One coach was said to hang "Team Jesus" banners in the locker room and another to lead athletes in prayer, evoking Jesus' name regularly. Other complaints involved the lack of accommodation for Jewish cadets to observe their Sabbath or to observe holy days because major military events were/are scheduled at the same time. Nevertheless, some junior and senior Jewish cadets "felt that things have gotten better [since 2004] and religious/cultural demeaning jokes and slurs have become less frequent."[15]

Some groups and individuals in the armed forces claim they face outright discrimination. That is the argument from atheists who contend that they are condemned for their *non*belief in a supernatural or supreme being. Master Sgt. Kathleen Johnson, who founded the Military Association of Atheists and Freethinkers (MAAF), reports to *Newsweek*: "Before I got to be the rank I am I had to keep my head down and my mouth shut. I had commanding officers who made it clear that they wouldn't tolerate atheism in their ranks."[16]

It is common for some military chaplains and commanders to repeat the old saying "there are no atheists in foxholes," meaning that soldiers who are atheists, agnostics, and freethinkers automatically will turn to God when their lives are in danger. The maxim, which dates from World War II, also infers that atheists are unpatriotic cowards who cannot be counted on to fight for their country. MAAF adamantly disagrees with that myth and declares, "Nonbelievers are serving, and have served, in our nation's military with distinction!"[17] In fact, the organization sponsored a rally in Washington, DC, on Veterans Day 2005 to recognize the service of "atheists in foxholes," and it also maintains a website for the same purpose.

Wiccans make up another group of soldiers who have faced discrimination. Some have been prevented from practicing their religious beliefs, which include worship of the earth and nature and celebrating the seasons. The DoD estimates that there are about 1,900 active-duty Wiccans in the armed forces, but military chaplains who are Wiccans are not welcome. The DoD contends that there are too few Wiccans in the military to warrant a chaplain, but the *Washington Post* reports: "Among the nearly 2,900 clergy on active duty are . . . 22 rabbis for 4,038 Jews, 11 imams for 3,386 Muslims, six teachers for 636 Christian Scientists, and one Buddhist chaplain for 4,546 Buddhists."[18] Wiccans who have tried to become chaplains have been turned down. In 2006, when Donald Larsen "applied to become the first Wiccan chaplain in the U.S. armed forces . . . his superiors not only denied his request but also withdrew him from Iraq and removed him from the chaplain corps."[19] Before he became a Wiccan, Larsen had been a Pentecostal Christian minister in Iraq, but that changed after a twelve-hundred-year old mosque was bombed, and Sunni and Shiite attacks on each other forced him to think about the continued violence "in the name of God." As he told a *Washington Post* reporter:

> When you think back over the Catholic–Protestant conflict, how the Jews have suffered, how some Christians justified slavery, the Crusades, and now the fighting between Shiite and Sunni Muslims, I just decided I'm done. . . . I will not be part of any church that unleashes its clergy to preach that particular individuals or faith groups are damned.[20]

Another discriminatory act against Wiccans in the military prompted a lawsuit. It came about because Roberta Stewart and Karen DePolito, widows of Wiccan military personnel, applied for the Wiccan pentacle symbol (a five-pointed star inside a circle) to be engraved on their husbands' headstones. Stewart's husband was killed in Afghanistan in 2005, and DePolito's husband was a Korean War veteran who died in 2006. Similar Wiccan petitions had been pending since the mid-1990s. Because of the long wait for action on the applications, Americans United for Separation of Church and State and several Wiccan congregations sued the VA in November 2006. The suit sought inclusion of the pentacle on the VA's accepted list of religious symbols. The VA settled the suit in April 2007 by placing the pentacle on the list of symbols that can be engraved free of charge on military headstones.

NOTES

1. Quoted in Regina Medina, "Army Recruiters Deny 3 Hopefuls," *Philadelphia Daily News*, August 2, 2006, www.sldn .org/templates/press/record.html?section=5&record=3097 (accessed June 23, 2007).

2. U.S. Army, "Army Profile FY2005," *Army Demographics*, p. 4, www.armyg1.army.mil/hr/demographics/FY05%20Army% 20Profile.pdf (accessed June 23, 2007).

3. United States Army Signal Center, Fort Gordon, GA, "Hello Girls," May 5, 2006, www.gordon.army.mil/OCOS/Museum/ hlogrl.asp (accessed March 31, 2007).

4. United States Army Signal Center, "Hello Girls."

5. Daniel de Vise, "Defense Dept. Surveys Academy Sex Assaults," *Washington Post*, March 19, 2005, p. A1.

6. U.S. Army Sexual Assault Prevention and Response Program, n.d., www.sexualassault.army.mil (accessed June 23, 2007).

7. "No Tolerance for Sexual Assault," *Air Force News*, April 5, 2007, www.military.com/features/0,15240,131257,00.html (accessed June 23, 2007).

8. Helen Benedict, "The Private War of Women Soldiers," Salon.com, March 7, 2007, www.salon.com/news/feature/2007/03/ 07/women_in_military (accessed June 23, 2007).

9. U.S. Army Sexual Assault Prevention and Response Program, "FAQs," 2005, www.sexualassault.army.mil/content/faqs.cfm (accessed January 4, 2008).

10. U.S. Army Sexual Assault Prevention and Response Program, "FAQs."

11. Quoted in Medina, "Army Recruiters Deny 3 Hopefuls."

12. Daniel Gallington, "Carefully Drawn Line," *Washington Times*, March 21, 2007, www.potomacinstitute.org/media/mediaclips/2007/Gallington_WT_032107.pdf (accessed June 23, 2007).

13. Michael Kowalski profile, *Careers in the Military*, n.d., www.careersinthemilitary.com/index.cfm?fuseaction=main.careerpath&mc_id=65 (accessed June 20, 2007).

14. Headquarters, U.S. Air Force, *The Report of the Headquarters Review Group Concerning the Religious Climate at the U.S. Air Force Academy*, June 22, 2005, www.af.mil/pdf/HQ_Review_Group_Report.pdf (accessed April 12, 2007).

15. Rebecca Phillips, "Atheist Soldiers Demand to Be Recognized," *Newsweek*, August 21, 2006, p. 18.

16. Phillips, "Atheist Soldiers."

17. Phillips, "Atheist Soldiers."

18. Alan Cooperman, "The Army Chaplain Who Wanted to Switch to Wicca? Transfer Denied," *Washington Post*, February 19, 2007, p. C1.

19. Cooperman, "Army Chaplain."

20. Cooperman, "Army Chaplain."

8 Conscientious Objectors

During past wars involving the United States, the federal government has enforced selective service laws requiring a draft, or compulsory military service for young men (women are exempt). But many who believed strongly that they could not participate in armed conflict applied for conscientious objector (CO) status, a legal exemption from the armed forces that allows COs to provide alternative services, such as hospital work. Most of the people who have objected to America's wars have been members of traditional peace churches, such as Brethren, Quakers, Mennonites, Moravians, and Shakers. Other religious objectors have included people of Catholic, Jewish, and Muslim faiths.

Until World War II, CO status was limited to the religious, but the first U.S. peacetime draft law passed in October 1940, more than a year before Pearl Harbor, no longer required that a person belong to a traditional peace church in order to register as a CO. Those who objected to war and killing on the basis of strongly held ethical, humanitarian, and philosophical principles could obtain CO standing. If COs were willing to do alternative service, they could provide noncombat duty in the armed forces or take part in a program called Civilian Public Service (CPS). At CPS camps established by the U.S. government and peace churches, civilians were in charge rather than the military. During World War II, more than 37,000 COs provided alternative service in the armed forces or in the CPS camps.

"Just because we volunteered, doesn't mean we volunteered to throw our lives away for nothing. You can only push human beings so far."

—Marc Train, a nineteen-year-old soldier who went AWOL to participate in an antiwar demonstration in Washington, DC, in March 2007[1]

ATTITUDES TOWARD COs

In every war, there have been people who have expressed contempt for COs. During the Civil War, COs obtained legal status for the first time, but attitudes toward and treatment of them varied from tolerance to death by firing squad. President Lincoln, for example, established a policy that allowed religious pacifists to serve in hospitals or to educate freed slaves. In the Confederacy, there was little lenience for those who refused to fight.

According to Howard Zinn, some World War I COs working in alternative service jobs at army bases "were often treated with sadistic brutality."[2] In his book *A People's History of the United States: 1492–Present*, Zinn explains how three men who refused to do any combat or noncombat service were brutalized:

> A hemp rope slung over the railing of the upper tier was put about their necks, hoisting them off their feet until they were at the point of collapse. Meanwhile the officers punched them on their ankles and shins. They were then lowered and the rope was tied to their arms, and again they were hoisted off their feet. This time a garden hose was played on their faces with a nozzle about six inches from them, until they collapsed completely.[3]

VIETNAM AND ANTIWAR SENTIMENT

After World War II, the draft continued until 1975 through periods of peace and armed conflict. It was a particularly contentious issue during the U.S. active participation in the Vietnam War (1964–1975). Numerous college students were opposed to the draft, especially when President Lyndon Johnson's administration established a policy to make students with low grades some of the first to be eligible for conscription.

Perhaps no American war since the Civil War has created more division. The Vietnam War split families and the nation into two camps: those who believed in the stated purpose of

CO AND ANTIWAR PROTESTOR DAVID DELLINGER

David Dellinger (1915–2004) was not a likely CO. He grew up in an affluent family, part of what was considered "new-world royalty" in Boston, Massachusetts. From an early age, Dellinger questioned the conservative views of his father, whom he admired and respected. He became increasingly disillusioned about people of high social class—including his father—who would not speak out for justice. After he enrolled in Yale University at the age of seventeen, Dellinger became a social activist. The young collegian would often dress in his poorest clothes and take to the streets near the university to discover firsthand what it was like to be homeless, hungry, and desperate.

In 1940, he was exempt from the draft because he was a divinity student, but he refused to register with the selective service as was required by federal law. He was promised the directorship of a CO camp if he would follow that legally acceptable path. He still refused to register. He determined that to do so was to work in complicity with a system that had little moral accountability. He was sentenced to a year and a day in federal prison in Danbury, Connecticut, for breaking the law.

Dellinger married soon after his release and started the Peoples Peace Now Committee in 1943. That group led an antiwar protest demonstration in the nation's capital. He was arrested weeks later when the federal government cited him for refusing to take his Selective Service physical. He received a two-year sentence.

Dellinger's commitment to nonviolence and pacifism made him a leader of the antiwar movement that continued throughout most of his life. He chronicled much of his work in his 1993 book *From Yale to Jail: The Life Story of a Moral Dissenter*. He died in 2004. In remembrance, Colman McCarthy, director of the Washington, DC, Center for Teaching Peace, Inc., called Dellinger an "icon of nonviolence."[4]

the armed conflict—to stop the spread of communism in Asia—and those who denounced U.S. intervention in Vietnam's civil war. As would be expected, the latter group included many COs as well as a great number of pacifists. In addition, citizens in the United States began to turn against

A FAMOUS CO: MUHAMMAD ALI

Given the name Cassius Clay at birth in 1942, Muhammad Ali's story has been told countless times: his development as a boxer during high school; his flamboyant and boastful manner; his challenge to heavyweight champion Sonny Liston; his conversion to Islam while he was in his twenties; his name change to Muhammad Ali. One of the most famous incidents of his life, however, was his refusal to be inducted into the army when he was drafted in 1967. Ali's CO claim was ignored because the federal government did not recognize the Nation of Islam as a religion or its antiwar doctrine. Yet Ali remained loyal to his faith and declared:

> When I was asked to stand up and be sworn into the service, I thought about all the black people who'd been here for 400 years—all the lynching, raping and killing they'd suffered—and there was an Army fellow my age acting like God and telling me to go to Viet Nam and fight Asians who'd never called me Nigger, had never lynched me, had never put dogs on me—and outside I had millions of black people waiting to see what I was going to do. . . . I couldn't take that step because I knew the war was wrong, it was against my religious beliefs, and I was willing to go to jail for those beliefs.[5]

Convicted of draft evasion, Ali faced five years in prison. He appealed, but his boxing license was suspended in almost every state in the union. He lost his titles and most of his money. In 1971, the U.S. Supreme Court overturned his draft evasion conviction.

the war as they watched TV news programs that showed the brutal fighting, devastation, and the mounting dead in Vietnam. The antiwar movement built momentum in the mid-1960s. On college campuses and elsewhere, draft cards and U.S. flags were burned. Activists held rallies, teach-ins, and marches protesting the war. A huge antiwar protest took place at the Pentagon in Washington, DC, in 1967.

During the Vietnam conflict, there were more than 200,000 COs. Some of the young men eligible for the draft fled to Canada to escape conscription, and some young men already in the armed forces began to question their own participation in the military. One example was John Douglas Marshall, who was a University of Virginia student and member of the ROTC during the late 1960s. He was the grandson of S. L. A. Marshall, a prominent writer and brigadier general in the army reserves. John Marshall admired and loved his grandfather and hoped the elder Marshall would be proud of him.

During the young Marshall's first year in service, he began to doubt the reasons for the war and war itself. He studied pacifism and nonviolence and "applied to leave the army as a conscientious objector," according to Christian G. Appy's book of interviews, *Patriots: The Vietnam War Remembered from All Sides*.[6] When John Marshall's CO application was approved, he informed his family. His father refused to communicate with him for a year, and his grandfather disowned him. He never saw his grandfather again; he died in 1977. John Marshall did not go to his grandfather's funeral because he did not believe he would be welcome.[7]

CONTEMPORARY COs

Although the draft has not been in effect since 1973, young men between the ages of eighteen and twenty-five are required to register with the Selective Service. At that time, they may apply for classification as a CO and would be required to meet with the local Selective Service board to explain their beliefs and how those beliefs have influenced their lives. Based on the registrant's statements and written or personal testimonials of chaplains and others, the local board decides whether to grant or deny a CO classification.

According to a flyer from the Selective Service System headquartered in Washington, DC:

> Conscientious Objectors opposed to serving in the military will be placed in the Selective Service Alternative Service Program. This program attempts to match COs with local employers. Many types of jobs are available, however the job

must be deemed to make a meaningful contribution to the maintenance of the national health, safety, and interest. Examples of Alternative Service are jobs in:

- **conservation**
- **caring for the very young or very old**
- **education**
- **health care**

Length of service in the program will equal the amount of time a man would have served in the military, usually 24 months.[8]

Organizations that help young men with CO claims include the Central Committee for Conscientious Objectors, GI Rights Hotline, American Friends (Quakers) Service Committee, Center on Conscience and War, Committee Opposed to Militarism and the Draft, and numerous peace fellowships affiliated with religious organizations.

What about military personnel who no longer believe they can serve in the armed forces? Can they make a CO claim? They can and do. Consider the case of Robert Zabala, a University of California, Santa Cruz, student who joined the Marine Corps in 2003. During boot camp, he had a change of heart about killing and how recruits are desensitized to violence. He recalls that recruits were required to chant "kill, kill, kill" while practicing how to slit someone's throat with a knife. The constant killing practice; his instructors' display of "blood-lust," as Zabala describes it; and the constant propaganda messages about blowing up Iraqis convinced Zabala he could not be part of the armed forces.[9] He consulted with chaplains and psychologists and applied for CO status, which was denied. His platoon commander insisted Zabala was not sincere and knew very well that he would be trained to kill. Zabala took his case to court, and at the end of March 2007, "a federal judge in Northern California overruled the military justice system, ordering the Marine Corps to discharge Zabala as a conscientious objector within 15 days," according to the Interpress Service.[10]

A QUAKER IN THE MILITARY

Quakers are known for their antiwar beliefs and their peace efforts, but some Quakers do enlist or in earlier times were drafted. A young Quaker in the air force noted in 2004 that he was not able to join his faith group while in basic training but that he "chose to join. . . . I'm in Intelligence so I possibly may even be able to stop the killing before it happens. When chaplains ask about Quakers 'Peace Testimony,' I will openly admit the only order I probably could not follow would be to shoot someone. I just trust God to not allow me to be put in such a situation."[11]

A different outcome awaited twenty-two-year-old Army National Guard Specialist Katherine Jashinski, who had applied for CO status in 2003; after 18 months, her discharge as a CO was denied. In late 2005, she was scheduled to deploy to Afghanistan but refused to go and in a public statement explains that at age nineteen she had "enlisted in the Guard as a cook because I wanted to experience military life." She "believed that killing was immoral, but also that war was an inevitable part of life." Her views began to change, however, and she developed a strong belief in nonviolence and noted that she would "exercise my every legal right not [to] pick up a weapon" or to take part in any war effort. She concludes by noting that conscientious objectors are willing "to face adversity and uphold their values at any cost. We do this not because it is easy or popular, but because we are unable to do otherwise."[12]

In May 2006, Jashinski received a bad conduct discharge. She served a jail sentence of 120 days. Her statement and story appear on CO and antiwar websites.

NOTES

1. Quoted in Sarah Olson, "Another Soldier AWOL Rather Than Deploying to Iraq," Truthout, April 19, 2007, www.truthout.org/docs_2006/041907N.shtml (accessed June 23, 2007).

2. Howard Zinn, *A People's History of the United States: 1492–Present* (New York: HarperCollins, 2003), p. 371.

3. Zinn, *People's History*, p. 371.

4. Quoted in Patricia Sullivan, "Lifelong Protestor David Dellinger Dies," *Washington Post*, May 27, 2004, p. B7.

5. John D. McCallum, *The Encyclopedia of World Boxing Champions* (Radnor, PA: Chilton Book Company, 1975), p. 73.

6. Christian G. Appy, *Patriots: The Vietnam War Remembered from All Sides* (New York: Penguin Books, 2003), pp. 328–29.

7. Appy, *Patriots*, pp. 328–29.

8. *Selective Service System: Fast Facts*, last updated April 30, 2002, www.sss.gov/FSconsobj.htm (accessed June 20, 2007).

9. Aaron Glantz, "Civilian Court Sides with 'Conscientious Objector,'" April 5, 2007, ipsnews.net/news.asp?idnews=37233 (accessed June 23, 2007).

10. Glantz, "Civilian Court Sides with 'Conscientious Objector.'"

11. Miles B. posting on Beliefnet forum, January 16, 2004, www.beliefnet.com/boards/message_list.asp?boardID=33233&discussionID=248538 (accessed April 10, 2007).

12. Aidan Delgado, School of the Americas Watch, "First Female Conscientious Objector Sentenced for Refusing Deployment to Afghanistan," Press Release, May 24, 2006; see also Katherine Jashinski and Courage to Resist, "First Woman GI Takes Public Stand against War!" November 22, 2005, www.envirosagainstwar

.org/know/read.php?itemid=3446 (accessed June 18, 2007); Katherine Jashinski and Marisa Handler, "Army SPC Katherine Jashinski Speaks Out against War at Fort Benning, Georgia," Not in Our Name, November 17, 2005, www.notinourname.net/troops/ jashinski.htm (accessed June 18, 2007); Citizen Soldier, "Woman GI Publicly Stands against War as She Faces Immediate Deployment to Middle East," November 17, 2005, www.citizen-soldier.org/ katherinejashinski.html (accessed June 18, 2007).

In the War Zone

What's it like to face death and kill the enemy or perhaps innocent people? Americans in the armed forces during wars (past and present) have filled millions of pages and electronic files describing their experiences. Some accounts were written when there were lulls in the fighting; others were written as memoirs months or years after wars ended. Diaries, letters, and interviews with military personnel as well as citizens on the home front tell stories about how people have dealt with war throughout American history. Battle tactics and locations, weapons, and fighting forces obviously have changed over the years, but there has been one constant said to have been articulated by Union Army General William Tecumseh Sherman: "War is hell." And many war stories wherever and whenever they have been written or told testify to that fact.

"I've got a terrible feeling there's gonna be something tonight."
"We have a soldier down looks critical."
—Anonymous comments from the Iraq War documentary *Gunner Palace*[1]

"WAR IS HELL"

During the American Revolution, fighting battles was just part of war's hell. One of the greatest threats to soldiers was smallpox. Jeremiah Greenman, a seasoned soldier at the age of eighteen, noted in his diary (with his spelling and grammar) that it was a "very unwholesum time . . . very sickley. the men comes into town from head quarters . . . very plenty smallpox."[2]

John Greenwood's military account of the Revolutionary War also tells of the many who were sick with smallpox—the majority of his unit. Like others in the Continental army, the men never had enough rations and clothing, and many were "nearly dead with sickness and fatigue."[3] Early in the war, fifteen-year-old Greenwood was with a regiment on its way by "open boat," as he describes it, to Fort Ticonderoga on Lake Champlain in northern New York. As he reports:

> On the route, the rations served up to us each day, consisted of a pint of flour and a quarter-pound of pork for every man, and to cook this we were allowed to land at noon. We were without camp-kettles or any utensils whatever to make bread in, and pretty kind of stuff was the preparation . . . mixed up with water from the lake, by fellows as lousy, itchy, and nasty as hogs . . . when made and baked upon a piece of bark, so black with dirt and smoke I do not think a dog could eat it. But with us it went down, lice, itch, and all, without any grumbling, while the pork was broiled on a wooden fork and the drippings caught by the beautiful flour cakes.[4]

Soldiers not only suffered from poor diet and disease but also from exposure to freezing temperatures that could cause death. Greenwood narrowly escaped that fate while on a march. As he reports, "During the whole night [of the trek,] it alternately hailed, rained, snowed, and blew tremendously. I recollect very well that at one time when we halted on the road, I sat down on the stump of a tree and was so benumbed with cold that I wanted to go to sleep; had I been passed unnoticed I should have frozen to death without knowing it."[5] Greenwood was saved by a sergeant who got him up and walking again.

Anyone who reads or watches movies and videos about the American Civil War will find ample stories detailing the horrors of the four-year conflict that took hundreds of thousands of lives. One Union army soldier, John McClure, from Indiana was with General Ulysses S. Grant's forces in Virginia and told about a battle in a wooded area and his reaction to death:

> I hid behind a tree and looked out. Across the way, near enough for me to see, was a Rebel aiming at me. I put my hat

on a stick I'd picked up and stuck it out from behind the tree—as bait. Then I saw him peep out of the thicket and I shot him. It was the first time I'd ever seen the man I killed, and it was an awful feeling. I went to him and rolled him over. He was young. . . . He gave one groan and died. I had thought I might get his papers out of his wallet and let his folks at home know—but when I saw his face and heard him groan, I hadn't even the heart to do that.[6]

As the Civil War progressed, deaths from injuries and disease far outnumbered those who died in battle. At the time, medical personnel had only minimal training and little understanding of infection and disease and the effects of unsanitary conditions. On both sides, camps were notoriously filthy with decomposing garbage, nearby pits of human waste, and river water contaminated with bodies. Viruses and bacterial illness spread quickly. Typhoid fever, diarrhea, dysentery, pneumonia, and tuberculosis were common among the soldiers. Childhood contagious diseases also swept through some Civil War camps because there were so many susceptible young soldiers, especially those between the ages of fifteen and eighteen who had never before been exposed to such diseases as measles and chicken pox.

Recollections of being in a war zone have been common topics for those who have survived other conflicts. For example, many World War II veterans have shared their stories. As one Navy veteran writes:

When I finished high school in 1943 all the guys in my class accepted that the thing to do was join up to defeat the Japanese who had bombed Pearl Harbor more than a year before. There was no question in our minds—we wanted to defend our country.

I joined the Navy. I learned later that my training was excellent because I was prepared for what I would face in active service. . . . Soon after our LST [landing ship tank] set sail for the Asiatic-Pacific Theater of Operations, we were called to general quarters because of enemy bombers overhead. We had practiced the drill for weeks before and all

CARING FOR THE WOUNDED

Those who were injured during early wars were lucky to live through their treatment. One witness to the care of the Civil War wounded was teenager Tillie Pierce. She was born in 1848 and lived in Gettysburg. During the 1863 Battle of Gettysburg, Tillie with neighbors fled to the Jacob Wickert safe house on a hilltop several miles from Gettysburg while the Pierces stayed in town. Tillie Pierce later wrote about what she saw: "I fairly shrank back aghast at the awful sight presented. The approaches were crowded with wounded, dying and dead. The air was filled with moanings, and groanings. As we passed on toward the house, we were compelled to pick our steps in order that we might not tread on the prostrate bodies."[7] Pierce and her neighbors went into the house, which she wrote was "completely filled with the wounded." The tasks ahead of them seemed overwhelming and they "hardly knew what to do or where to go."[8] After Mrs. Weiker brought out whatever muslin and linen she could get by without, the group began to tear the cloth to make bandages for the wounded.

Outside the house, doctors had set up amputating benches. Pierce reported:

I must have become inured to seeing the terrors of battle, else I could hardly have gazed upon the scenes now presented. I was looking out of the windows facing the front yard. Near the basement door, and directly underneath the window I was at, stood one of these benches. I saw them lifting the poor men upon it, then the surgeons sawing and cutting off arms and legs, then again probing and picking bullets from the flesh.

I saw the surgeons hastily put a cattle horn over the mouths of the wounded ones, after they were placed upon the bench. . . . That was their mode of administrating chloroform, in order to produce unconsciousness. But the effect in some instances were not produced; for I saw the wounded throwing themselves wildly about, and shrieking with pain while the operation was going on.

To the south of the house, and just outside of the yard, I noticed a pile of limbs higher than the fence. It was a ghastly sight![9]

OFF THE SHELF

Personal narratives of young people at war are included in numerous books. By reading a few, you can gain some insight into the hardships, loneliness, fear, and brutalities that those on the front line have faced. Yvonne Latty's book *We Were There: Voices of African American Veterans from World War II to the War in Iraq* is a good example. One of the "voices" in the book comes from Stephen Hopkins, who enlisted in the army at age eighteen just before the beginning of the Korean War. In Korea, he was in battle and was captured by the Chinese; along with others, he was marched from Korea to China. Hopkins reports:

> We marched from winter to spring, and it was so cold. I always thought they were going to get tired of carrying us around and shoot us. By the time we made it to the prison camp, we were burying two or three guys a day. Out of three hundred guys, only about a hundred were left. The guys were dying of just about everything. I was always scared. You never knew if you were going to be taken somewhere and be shot. A couple of guys tried to escape, and you saw the Chinese bash their heads in or shoot them.[10]

on board responded well. As I completed my assigned duty, I thought "This is for *real*, I could be *killed*!" I wanted to be any place but in the Pacific Ocean.[11]

Robert Yancey, a veteran of three wars, was drafted as a teenager in World War II. He also served in the Korean and Vietnam Wars. On the front lines in Korea, "you had to dig in and make sure you knew where the enemy was located," he reports. He continues, "Before you kicked off an attack, everybody fired machine guns, mortars, everything you had." But, he adds, the "North Koreans and Chinese were like ants. . . . They came in like a plague. . . . The Chinese would take five hundred men and go over barbed wire, go through firepower, mines, and booby traps."[12]

GREETINGS FROM IRAQ!

No frontline communications have made use of the Internet like messages that have come from the war zones in Iraq and Afghanistan. E-mail and blogging (online diaries) reveal a myriad of emotions from those on the front lines. Most messages are sent to family and friends and frequently to newspapers, former schools, members of the U.S. Congress, and colleagues. In addition, video documentaries produced since 2003 feature the voices and experiences of frontline warriors. Only a few examples can be included here.

Nineteen-year-old Holly McGeoph was a light-truck mechanic in Iraq. In early January 2004, she sent an e-mail message home describing how she drove out with her section and they thought they spotted an improvised explosive device (IED). She backed up their vehicle to take a look. It turned out to be a false alarm, and McGeoph admits she was somewhat embarrassed, but in hasty e-mail style, she writes, "i knew we had done the rite thing. . . . i have full confidence in the people that I work with that if anybody's life was in danger that they would do everything in their power to not let anything happen, i know that i would do it for them in a heart beat."[13] Not long after her message was sent, McGeoph was killed by a roadside bomb that exploded near her Humvee.

Marine Major James McGarrahan was in Iraq in 2004 and in charge of eighteen marines, a navy corpsman, and a British civilian contractor. Their job was to run an Iraqi National Guard training center. The major reported to family members via e-mail that he was headquartered in

> an old Special Republican Guard camp on the outskirts of the town of Ramadi . . . the capital city of the Al-Anbar Province, home of the notorious "Sunni Triangle." From the rooftop parapets, we can clearly make out the houses and mosques on the edge of town. . . . On two sides of the camp are Iraqi farm fields, with some pomegranate and date palm orchards. An Iraqi farm is very similar to an American farm—a clothesline stretches between posts, a scruffy mutt lazes in the shade of a

tree, children play games in the yard while their parents tend rows of withered vegetables. When you're in uniform and bearing arms all day, it's important to keep in the back of your mind that just down the same road you walk on is a local citizen who's simply trying to . . . piece together something that resembles a normal life. . . .

The most challenging part of the job is communicating—my native translator was apprehended and executed by the Muj [mujahideen, or guerrilla fighters], and I am having a tough time learning Arabic on the fly. . . . My Iraqi counterpart [has] endless patience for teaching me Arabic.[14]

Details of the war zone in Ramadi appear in a letter printed in *Time* magazine. The letter was meant for family and friends but circulated among Pentagon and government officials. After verifying who wrote the letter, *Time* published it anonymously (at the author's request) in the magazine's October 2006 issue. The author notes that Ramadi was the "worst city in al-Anbar Province," adding

Lots and lots of insurgents killed in there since we arrived. . . . Every day is a nasty gun battle. They blast us with giant bombs in the road, snipers, mortars and small arms. We blast them with tanks, attack helicopters, artillery, our snipers (much better than theirs), and every weapon that an infantryman can carry. . . . We have as many attacks out here in the west as Baghdad. Yet, Baghdad has 7 million people, we have just 1.2 million. Per capita, al-Anbar province is the most violent place in Iraq by several orders of magnitude.[15]

In April 2007, *Newsweek* magazine published a special issue titled *Voices of the Fallen*. It contains excerpts from e-mails and letters that fallen soldiers in Iraq had sent to family and friends, who gave permission to print the correspondence. In one e-mail, Michael Mundell describes what it was like in Fallujah in mid-2006:

We continue to get mortared, with an occasional RPG [grenade launcher] shot at us thrown in for fun. . . . A little

GUNNER PALACE (A DOCUMENTARY ON DVD)

In late 2003 and early 2004, the U.S. Army's 2/3 Field Artillery Division (known as the Gunners) had taken over the bomb-damaged palace that once belonged to Saddam Hussein's son Uday. Soldiers called their base in the heart of Baghdad "Gunner Palace," and filmmaker Michael Tucker lived with the troops for two months, producing a film that one reviewer called a "living, unfinished document of a complicated war and the complicated young men who are fighting it."

The documentary takes the viewer along on raids and patrols, presents some humorous moments with jokes and clowning around at a pool party, and shows poignant scenes of troops relating to Iraqi children. Throughout the film, young soldiers tell about their experiences through hip-hop, in-your-face comments, and dialogue with one another.

girl was killed yesterday in a cross fire between our Iraqis, the Marines and the bad guys. Sad. . . .

We seem to be doing little, the city is mostly trash, rubble and AIF [anti-Iraq forces], and frankly I am tired of being a walking bull's-eye for anyone with an AK and nothing better to do, which includes most of the populace, apparently. We have found three IEDs before they could explode under our trucks. . . .

People are dying like flies here and I am sick of it.[16]

"TAPS"

Playing the twenty-four notes of "Taps" is one of the most recognized rituals of a military funeral, and the ceremony has been incorporated in memorial services and used in numerous films. It began during the Civil War as a lights-out call, a traditional signal called "Extinguish Lights" that had been passed on from the French. Sometimes the call was tapped out on drums when a bugler was not available.

In 1862 when the Army of the Potomac was at Harrison's Landing in Virginia, Brigadier General Daniel Butterfield asked his twenty-two-year-old brigade bugler, Private Oliver Wilcox Norton, to arrange a call based on a tune that the general whistled. Norton jotted the notes on an envelope, and after several trials, he played an arrangement that pleased the general. When other brigades heard the tune, they, too, adopted the call. By the end of 1863, Butterfield's tune became the official call for ending the day: "Put out the lights. Go to sleep."

The custom of playing "Taps" at burials also began during the Civil War—at the interment of a Union soldier whose battery was close to the front. Soldiers could not fire the customary three rifle shots over the grave because that might signal to Confederate soldiers that an attack was imminent. Thus, a solemn rendition of "Taps" was sounded, and the practice became a ritual at all burial services for Union soldiers. Confederates soon followed the example. By 1891, the tune was a standard part of military funerals. Today, a bugler plays the familiar song at the end of a military burial ceremony and is part of wreath-laying and memorial services.

U.S. Marine Corps Sgt. Stefan Schpuntow plays "Taps" during a memorial service for Marine Corps First Lt. Travis L. Manion at Camp Fallujah, Iraq, May 8, 2007. U.S. Marine Corps photo by Sgt. David J. Murphy.

Mundell was killed by an IED in Fallujah on January 5, 2007.

A message from Travis Youngblood was sent from Anbar Province and noted in part

> I've come so close to dying on at least 10 different occasions, I figure I can keep my luck, or whatever's working, up until I leave. I've had RPGs fly within inches of me. I've seen the guys they've hit. It blew them to pieces. We literally had to move rocks and debris to find hands, legs and other parts so we could send them home. I've had roadside bombs explode next to me, but they've been placed wrong, so I didn't get hurt. . . . I've been shot at countless times, I mean machinegun fire pinging and zipping past me. I had the goggles on my helmet shot.[17]

Youngblood died from injuries suffered in an IED explosion on July 21, 2005.

WAR STATISTICS

Personal stories are some of the most compelling ways to learn what it is like to be on the front lines of war or at the home front defending one's life and property. But figures compiled by the U.S. government provide a perspective—albeit an unemotional one—on the human cost of war. Statistics give an overview of how many have served in each of America's numerous wars, the number killed in battle, and those who have received nonmortal wounds. The data in table 9.1 are adapted from a U.S. Department of Veterans Affairs fact sheet.[18]

NOTES

1. *Gunner Palace*, DVD, produced by Petra Epperlein (New York: Palm Pictures, 2004).

2. Jeremiah Greenman, *Diary of a Common Soldier in the American Revolution: 1775–1783*, ed. Robert C. Bray and Paul E. Bushnell (DeKalb: Northern Illinois University Press, 1978), p. 73.

3. John Greenwood, *A Young Patriot in the American Revolution: 1775–1783* (Tyrone, PA: Westvaco, 1981), p. 78.

Table 9.1.   Numbers of U.S. Service Members and Casualties, 1775–June 2007

	Total U.S. Service Members	Deployed	Battle Deaths	Other Deaths (In Theater)	Other Deaths in Service (Nontheater)	Nonmortal Woundings
American Revolution (1775–1783)	217,000	N/A	4,435	N/A	N/A	6,188
War of 1812 (1812–1815)	286,730	N/A	2,260	N/A	N/A	4,505
Indian Wars (approx. 1817–1898)	106,000 (VA estimate)	N/A	1,000 (VA estimate)	N/A	N/A	N/A
Mexican War (1846–1848)	78,718	N/A	1,733	N/A	11,550	4,152
Civil War (Union) (1861–1865)	2,213,363	N/A	140,414	N/A	224,097	281,881
Civil War (Confederate) (1861–1865)	1,500,000	N/A	74,524	N/A	59,297*	N/A
Spanish-American War (1898–1902)	306,760 (worldwide)	N/A	385	N/A	2,061	1,662
World War I (1917–1918)	4,734,991 (worldwide)	N/A	53,402	N/A	63,114	204,002
World War II (1941–1945)	16,112,566 (worldwide)	N/A	291,557	N/A	113,842	671,846
Korean War (1950–1953)	5,720,000 (worldwide)	N/A	33,741	2,833	17,672	103,284
Vietnam War (1964–1975)	8,744,000 (worldwide)	3,403,000 (to Southeast Asia)	47,424	10,785	32,000	153,303
Desert Shield/ Desert Storm (1990–1991)	2,322,000 (worldwide)	694,550 (to Gulf)	147	235	1,590	467
America's Wars Total (1775–1991)	43,185,893 (during wartime)	N/A	653,708	14,560	525,930	1,447,281
Iraq and Afghanistan War**	3,573	N/A	N/A	N/A	N/A	25,950

*Does not include an estimated 26,000 to 31,000 who died in Union prisons.
** As of June 2007; an update is available on www.globalsecurity.org/military/ops/iraq_casualties.htm and www.antiwar.com/casualties.

109

4. Greenwood, *Young Patriot*, p. 78.

5. Greenwood, *Young Patriot*, pp. 77, 81.

6. Nancy Niblack Baxter, ed. and comp., *Hoosier Farmboy in Lincoln's Army: The Civil War Letters of Pvt. John R. McClure* (Indianapolis: Guild Press of Indiana, 1992), p. 55.

7. Matilda "Tillie" Pierce Alleman, *At Gettysburg; or, What a Girl Saw and Heard of the Battle: A True Narrative* (New York: W. Lake Borland, 1889), digital.library.upenn.edu/women/alleman/gettysburg/gettysburg.html (accessed June 23, 2007); see also "The Battle of Gettysburg, 1863," EyeWitness to History, www.eyewitnesstohistory.com/pfgtburg.htm (accessed June 23, 2007).

8. Alleman, *At Gettysburg*; "Battle of Gettysburg, 1863."

9. Alleman, *At Gettysburg*; "Battle of Gettysburg, 1863."

10. Quoted in Yvonne Latty, with photographs by Ron Tarver, *We Were There: Voices of African American Veterans, from World War II to the War in Iraq* (New York: HarperCollins, 2004), p. 64.

11. Arthur Gay, personal notes about World War II, April 2007.

12. Quoted in Latty, *We Were There*, p. 70.

13. "Letters Home from Iraq," *USA Today*, n.d., www.usatoday.com/news/graphics/letters_iraq/flash.htm (accessed June 23, 2007).

14. Major James McGarrahan, e-mail to the author, December 6, 2004.

15. "The Secret Letter from Iraq," *Time*, October 6, 2006, www.time.com/time/world/article/0,8599,1543658,00.html (accessed June 22, 2007).

16. Quoted in Jon Meacham, "Our Soldiers' Stories: The War in the Words of the Dead," Editorial, *Newsweek*, April 2, 2007, p. 24.

17. "A Glimmer of Hope," Correspondence of American Soldiers, Iraq War, *Newsweek*, April 2, 2007, p. 44.

18. United States Department of Veterans Affairs, "Fact Sheet: America's Wars," November 2006, www1.va.gov/opa/fact/amwars.asp (accessed April 25, 2007).

10 Life after the Military

Returning from war has certainly been a joyous occasion for many military personnel past and present. Balloons, flowers, flags, welcome-home signs, parades, bands, and parties have been part of homecoming celebrations for U.S. service people. Yet, many (but not all) veterans and their families have faced a variety of problems in their daily lives, such as difficulty reuniting with family and friends, getting adequate medical care for injuries and psychiatric problems, struggling to go back to work or find a job, and being or feeling alienated from the rest of society. Each war has brought its own set of trials for veterans.

In the case of Revolutionary War veterans, for example, the immediate problem was getting discharged from the armed forces at the end of hostilities. Some waited months to go home and frequently were without adequate clothing or shoes. Jeremiah Greenman, who in 1775 at age seventeen had enlisted, noted that his troops were "in a Miserable condition some of them not a Shoe or Stocking to their feet and the climate at this place much sevearer, than in the Estern States."[2] Eventually each soldier received only a pair of shoes before being released. Revolutionary veterans also had to wait for their pensions. Because the newly formed U.S. government lacked funds, only the most destitute received allotments. The federal government also was slow in paying pensions to veterans of later wars.

However, after every war, one of the most pressing issues for veterans has been adjusting to life at home. Perhaps the

> "The insanity of the war haunts you for the rest of your life, and the living sometimes aren't the lucky ones. They are the ones that are dying slower than others."
>
> **—An Iraq War veteran**[1]

most unfavorable public reactions to returning troops came during and after the Vietnam War.

VIETNAM VETERANS

The United States was so divided over the conflict in Vietnam that many soldiers who returned from the fighting were not celebrated or respected like veterans of other wars. Veterans were scapegoats for the anger and frustration that many Americans felt, equating military service with the hated actions of their government. Some were spit on, verbally insulted, and even physically attacked. A Nebraska soldier recalls, "When I came back from Vietnam I was dumb enough

TRIBAL HONORS

Although some Vietnam veterans were treated with hostility, that was not the case for Native Americans who returned to their tribal homes. As warriors they were, and still are, honored before joining the armed forces and after they return. They gain high status and a special place in their tribe's spiritual world. A Kiowa Vietnam veteran explains, "My people honored me as a warrior. We had a feast and my parents and grandparents thanked everyone who prayed for my safe return. We had a 'special' [dance] and I remembered as we circled the drum, I got a feeling of pride. I felt good inside because that's the way the Kiowa people tell you that you've done well."[3] And a Cherokee Vietnam veteran recalls,

After I got home, my uncles sat me down and had me tell them what it [the war] was all about. One of them had been in the service in World War II and knew what war was like. We talked about what went on over there, about killing and the waste, and one of my uncles said that God's laws are against war. They never talked about those kinds of things with me before.[4]

DID YOU KNOW?

Homelessness has become an increasing problem among Vietnam veterans. According to the Department of Veterans Affairs (VA), there are more homeless Vietnam-era veterans than the number of service people who died in that war. Nevertheless, the VA declares that even though many Vietnam veterans suffer from PTSD or other mental disorders, "studies do not suggest that there is a causal connection between military service, service in Vietnam, or exposure to combat and homelessness among veterans."[5] According to the VA:

> One-third of adult homeless men and nearly one-quarter of all homeless adults have served in the armed forces. While there is no true measure of the number of homeless veterans, it has been estimated that fewer than 200,000 veterans may be homeless on any given night and that twice as many veterans experience homelessness during a year. Many other veterans are considered at risk because of poverty, lack of support from family and friends and precarious living conditions in overcrowded or substandard housing. Ninety-seven percent of homeless veterans are male and the vast majority are single. About half of all homeless veterans suffer from mental illness and more than two-thirds suffer from alcohol or drug abuse problems. Nearly 40 percent have both psychiatric and substance abuse disorders.[6]

to wear my dress uniform in the San Francisco International Airport. This was on April 15, 1970. A nicely dressed woman in her twenties blocked my path and hissed 'God damned murderer' in my face."[7]

Then there was the experience of an eighteen-year-old African American who joined the marines and immediately after boot camp was sent to Vietnam. The first time he came home, he reports that he "drove across country with two white marines" and stopped for breakfast. "The waitress came up to us and asked to speak to one of the other guys. . . . The next thing we're leaving. The waitress told my friend that she didn't want to serve me. Being the Marines that they are, after all we had gone through, they weren't going to eat there either. I was shocked—I hadn't been back in the country twenty-four hours."[8]

The animosity toward Vietnam War veterans, whether due to prejudicial attitudes or loathing for the war, was only one of the problems they faced. Homecoming was especially difficult for those suffering terrible injuries—loss of limbs and brain damage—and emotional scars that have lasted for years. Many were filled with rage because of a war that seemed futile and resulted in unnecessary loss of life. Some drank and used drugs to ease the pain. Substance abuse sometimes led to loss of family, friends, jobs, and homes, which is also the case with veterans of later wars.

FROM "SHELL SHOCK" TO PTSD

During World War I, soldiers who experienced major traumatic events during battle developed a shaking disorder and partial paralysis, which was then called "shell shock," and during World War II complete exhaustion, known as "combat fatigue." After the Vietnam War, the psychological condition that veterans suffered became known as posttraumatic stress disorder (PTSD) and was officially recognized by mental health experts. It is a disorder that is seen in Gulf War and Iraq veterans.

Symptoms of PTSD "can include anxiety, restlessness, disturbed sleep, nightmares, irritability, outbursts of anger and hostile behavior," according to *Science Daily*.[9] The VA fact sheet notes that "approximately 317,000 veterans with a primary or secondary diagnosis of PTSD received treatment at VA medical centers and clinics in 2005." During the same year, the VA reports "more than 50,000 veterans received PTSD-related services at Vet Centers."[10] Some experts say that the percentage of Iraq and Afghanistan veterans suffering from PTSD is likely to exceed that of Vietnam veterans, as more and more soldiers are experiencing multiple tours of duty. There also are concerns that an increasing number of

Iraq veterans will turn to alcohol and other drugs to deal with their problems.

One example is Iraq veteran Chris Packley, whose inner battle with PTSD was described in several newspaper accounts. A former marine and top marksman on a sniper team, Packley was in his early twenties when he was sent to Fallujah. He returned home in 2004. As he explains to a reporter for the *Chicago Tribune*, "it started before I came home. I told the psychiatrist about it, but he didn't care or do nothing."[11] According to the report, "Packley couldn't sleep more than 45 minutes a night. In his dreams, he saw people get shot and saw himself shooting. A scene with two Iraqis holding two children in front of them as human shields would stir him awake, sweating."[12] He also had flashbacks of his twenty-year-old friend dying on the battlefield. Packley tried to drown his misery by drinking heavily and smoking marijuana. While still in the armed forces, he left the base without permission and got into fights. He was expelled from the marines and received an other-than-honorable (OTH) discharge. An OTH discharge is given when the conduct and performance of a member of the armed services seriously breaches what the military requires, such as committing violent acts or endangering the welfare of other members of the military. As a result, Packley lost his free counseling and medicine needed to treat his PTSD.[13]

Hundreds of soldiers with PTSD and other mental health problems have found themselves in similar predicaments. There has been little sympathy in the armed forces for misconduct related to mental health disorders, which some view as cowardly or phony acts. Members of the military are expected to be physically and emotionally capable of facing almost any war condition. When they don't meet these expectations, they may be discharged without treatment. In addition, active-duty soldiers with PTSD may not seek treatment because they fear that their military career or chances of future employment after discharge will be jeopardized. Also, they hesitate to go to a mental health clinic because of the stigma attached.

A study published in the *Archives of Internal Medicine* in March 2007 showed that veterans between the ages of eighteen and twenty-four "were at greatest risk for receiving mental health or posttraumatic stress disorder diagnoses compared with veterans 40 years or older." Although the study observes that "little is known about . . . mental health diagnoses among . . . veterans seen at VA facilities," it concludes that "early detection and intervention beginning in primary care settings are needed to prevent chronic mental illness and disability" among the Iraq veterans.[14]

TRANSITIONS TO CIVILIAN LIFE

Out of the tens of thousands of military personnel who return to civilian life each year, many have been able to make the transition successfully. As with veterans of earlier wars, men and women who have returned from the Iraq fighting have been able to enter the workforce or continue their education. Some have received job or educational assistance from their branch of service, the VA, or private organizations. The Department of Defense (DoD), state governments, and private employers also have helped through veteran job fairs, which are advertised frequently on the Internet or in other media.

Wounded Iraq War veterans who attended a DoD-sponsored job fair in San Antonio, Texas, in March 2007 included many amputees or those with severe burns or other battle injuries. They were recovering from their wounds at Fort Sam Houston and went to the fair looking for job possibilities after their discharge. Among them was twenty-one-year-old Chad Rozanski, who came in a wheelchair. He appreciated the opportunity the fair offered because he knew he wasn't "going to be continually turned down" for a job or have to explain repeatedly how he lost both of his legs due to an explosion in Iraq.[15] According to the Associated Press, employers at the fair reported that "veterans—wounded or otherwise—can be an asset. . . . They are disciplined, hardworking, capable of making decisions, and sometimes come with security clearance that is important for government agencies and DOD contractors."[16]

With the help of the Marine Corps, Cooper Brannan, another injured veteran of the Iraq War, has attempted to fulfill his dream career. Brannan, a twenty-two-year-old marine infantryman, had long wanted to be a professional baseball pitcher. While completing two tours in Iraq, he frequently practiced, playing catch with fellow marines between shifts on patrol and guard duty. He was evacuated home after a grenade blew off most of his little finger. The rest of his finger and part of his hand were amputated. Brannan's injury may seem insignificant compared to arm and leg amputees, but many people, including Brannan himself, thought his career aspirations were doomed. He was recovering from his injury at the Naval Medical Center in San Diego when he received an offer to try out for a pitching job with the San Diego Padres. The military ordered him to go play baseball. He was accepted by the Padres, and later he told the Associated Press his reaction to being inside the carpeted clubhouse with TVs, whirlpools, and plenty of food: "It's definitely a huge culture shock. . . . You go from living from the Bible times to coming back living in civilization, pretty much. . . . You appreciate the smaller things in life. . . . Being able to walk outside your house without feeling like a bomb is going to go off. . . . Being able to watch TV. Being able to use a toilet."[17]

Other Iraq veterans have attempted to pick up where they left off before going to war. Californian Paul Volpe, twenty-one years old, has done just that. He chose to join the Marine Corps right out of high school in 2003 rather than enroll in one of the three universities that had accepted him. After basic training and combat readiness, he was sent to Iraq and during his two years there took part in offensives against insurgents in Fallujah. He and his platoon were ambushed, and Volpe suffered serious injuries. After weeks of hospitalization and painful recovery, he was discharged in 2005 and was determined to get on with his education by enrolling at San

Diego State University. He told a reporter for the university's *360 Magazine*, "I want to experience it all. I don't want to miss out on anything just because I didn't go (to college). . . . I could have done it when I graduated high school, but I chose a different path.

DID YOU KNOW?

As of late 2007, about 23.5 million U.S. veterans were still alive, according to the VA. They included 3 World War I veterans who are more than 100 years old, about 2.4 million from World War II, and about the same number from the Korean War. VA statistics show that there are more than seven million Vietnam veterans and more than two million Desert Shield/Storm (Gulf War) veterans. Each month there are growing numbers of U.S. veterans of the so-called Global War on Terror—that is, the fight against groups who are not part of any national army but attack and terrorize civilians, government officials, and military personnel worldwide.[18]

Now it's time for me to get a good education, a valuable degree, and a good job."[19]

VETERANS FOR AND AGAINST THE IRAQ WAR

Like the Vietnam War, the fighting in Iraq has created heated arguments in the United States and abroad. While the vast majority of Americans have expressed their support for the nation's troops, there have been great divides regarding U.S. involvement in Iraq's civil strife. Along with American civilians and government officials, veterans who have come home from Iraq have become part of the controversy—speaking out for or against the war.

Some adamantly believe that the United States has a moral responsibility to spread democracy in the Middle East and that the U.S.-led invasion of Iraq was justified. To many, it's a religious crusade to save the world from evil. They have supported President George W. Bush's argument that the security of the civilized world depends on defeating terrorists in Iraq and that withdrawing from Iraq would bring chaos there and at home. Among national veterans organizations that have supported such a view are Veterans of Foreign Wars and the American Legion. In addition, citizen groups have organized to support the Iraq War, such as Move America Forward, Progress for America, Families United in Support of Our Troops and Their Mission, and some religious denominations.

Public support for the U.S.-led invasion of Iraq was high in 2003, but since then, there has been a downward slide in opinions about the war. In February 2007, the nonpartisan Pew Research Center found that a majority of Americans believed the war was not going well and wanted the U.S. troops to come home as soon as possible.

Those who have seen no justification for a war with a country that is not a clear danger to the United States have argued that invading Iraq was based on lie after lie. The veterans' groups involved include Iraq Veterans against the War, Veterans for Peace, Veterans for America, Votevets.org, and GI Hotline. Other organizations have connections with the military but are not composed primarily of veterans. Among them are West Point Graduates against the War, Military Families Speak Out, Service Academy Graduates against the War, and numerous peace groups.

NOTES

1. "Iraq War Vets Describe Life after the Conflict," *Today Show*, January 24, 2005, www.msnbc.msn.com/id/6860510 (accessed April 30, 2007).

2. Robert C. Bray and Paul F. Bushnell, eds., *Diary of a Common Soldier in the American Revolution, 1775–1783: An Annotated Edition of the Military Journal of Jeremiah Greenman* (DeKalb: Northern Illinois University Press, 1978), p. 270.

3. Quoted in "Native Americans and the U.S. Military," Frequently Asked Questions, Department of the Navy—Naval Historical Center, August 8, 2006, www.history.navy.mil/faqs/faq61-1.htm (accessed June 19, 2007).

4. Quoted in "Native Americans."

5. U.S. Department of Veterans Affairs, "Overview of Homelessness," October 12, 2006, www1.va.gov/homeless/page.cfm?pg=1 (accessed June 23, 2007).

6. U.S. Department of Veterans Affairs, "Fact Sheet: VA Programs for Homeless Veterans," September 2006, www1.va.gov/opa/fact/hmlssfs.asp (accessed June 23, 2007).

7. Quoted in Bob Greene, *Homecoming: When the Soldiers Returned from Vietnam* (New York: G. P. Putnam's Sons, 1989), p. 232.

8. Quoted in Yvonne Latty, with photographs by Ron Tarver, *We Were There: Voices of African American Veterans, from World War II to the War in Iraq* (New York: HarperCollins, 2004), p. 88.

9. "Traumatic Stress Disorder, Dementia Linked in WWII Vets," *Science Daily*, January 14, 2000, www.sciencedaily.com/releases/2000/01/000113233143.htm (accessed June 23, 2007).

10. U.S. Department of Veterans Affairs, "Fact Sheet: Veterans with Post-Traumatic Stress Disorder (PTSD)," March 2006, www1.va.gov/opa/fact/ptsd.asp (accessed June 22, 2007).

11. Jeremy Manier and Judith Graham, "Veterans Fight the War Within," *Chicago Tribune*, March 12, 2007, www.chicagotribune.com/news/nationworld/chi-070312ptsd,0,4597891.story (accessed June 23, 2007); see also Gregg Zoroya, "Troubled Troops in No-Win Fight," *USA Today*, November 2, 2006, www.usatoday.com/news/nation/2006-11-01-troubled-troops_x.htm (accessed June 23, 2007).

12. Manier and Graham, "Veterans Fight the War Within"; Zoroya, "Troubled Troops."

13. Manier and Graham, "Veterans Fight the War Within"; Zoroya, "Troubled Troops."

14. Karen H. Seal, Daniel Bertenthal, Christian R. Miner, Saunak Sen, and Charles Marmar, "Bringing the War Back Home," Abstract, *Archives of Internal Medicine*, March 12, 2007, archinte.ama-assn.org/cgi/content/abstract/167/5/476 (accessed June 23, 2007).

15. Michelle Roberts, "Wounded Vets Look to Life after Military at Job Fairs," Chron.com, March 28, 2007, www.diversityworking.com/communityChannels/veteran/newsPublish/story.php?id=1057 (accessed June 23, 2007).

16. Roberts, "Wounded Vets."

17. Quoted in "Wounded Iraq Vet Makes Major League Pitch," *CBS News*, March 5, 2007, www.cbsnews.com/stories/2007/03/05/ sportsline/main2537134.shtml (accessed June 23, 2007).

18. Department of Veterans Affairs, "America's Wars," November 2007, www1.va.gov/opa/fact/docs/amwars.pdf (accessed January 8, 2008).

19. Quoted in Aaron J. Hoskins, "Life after Iraq: From the Deserts of Iraq to the Halls of Montezuma," San Diego State University *360 Magazine*, Fall 2006, pp. 18–22, advancement.sdsu .edu/marcomm/360/images/360fall06.pdf (accessed June 23, 2007).

11 Working for Peace

Individuals and organizations working for peace have been active before and during most of America's wars. In colonial times, Quakers, the Amish, Hutterites, and other traditional religious peace groups opposed war and often were persecuted for it. Formal peace societies or organizations were not established until the 1800s, with such figures as Henry David Thoreau (1817–1862), known for his now-famous book *Walden* and his views on civil disobedience. Thoreau was arrested and jailed because he refused to pay taxes that supported the Mexican-American War, which he declared was waged by the United States for imperialist purposes.

Another early peace activist was Jeannette Rankin (1880–1973). She was the first woman elected to the U.S. Congress (a few other women filled vacancies left by the deaths of their husbands). Also, she was the only congressional member to vote against U.S. involvement in World War I. Her stand prompted harsh criticism—some called her a coward and traitor—and she was denounced by the press. But she did not back down, saying she wanted to stand by her country but could not vote for war: "I felt that the first time the first woman in Congress had a chance to say no to war, she should say it."[2] Saying no was not enough, however. As history records, the United States entered World War I and subsequent wars from World War II onward—in spite of protests from peace activists.

"I did everything I could. . . . I wrote letters and called Congressmen. I marched and held signs. So many other people did too. Then Bush said he wouldn't listen no matter what we did. I felt all our efforts were worthless."

—A Minnesota college student describing peace efforts before the United States invaded Iraq[1]

WHAT'S YOUR OPINION?

In 1963, President John F. Kennedy declared:

The United States, as the world knows, will never start a war. We do not want a war. We do not now expect a war. This generation of Americans has already had enough—more than enough—of war and hate and oppression. We shall be prepared if others wish it. We shall be alert to try to stop it. But we shall also do our part to build a world of peace where the weak are safe and the strong are just. We are not helpless before that task or hopeless of its success. Confident and unafraid, we labor on—not toward a strategy of annihilation but toward a strategy of peace.[3]

How well do you think the United States has labored on "toward a strategy of peace"? What's your opinion?

One of the most effective antiwar efforts occurred during the Vietnam era, when the public, media, and congressional members increasingly pressed both Presidents Johnson and Nixon to withdraw and troops were brought home. In addition, peace activists have "played a major role in preventing . . . nuclear war," according to Lawrence S. Wittner, professor of history at the State University at Albany, New York.[4] He points out that the "peace movement's struggle against the nuclear arms race and its clearest manifestation, nuclear testing, led directly to" President John F. Kennedy's 1963 commencement speech at American University.[5] Kennedy called on the Soviet Union to work with

To help promote goodwill, a U.S. Army soldier gives school supplies and other humanitarian assistance to children in Afghanistan, April 30, 2007. Photo by Staff Sgt. Michael Bracken, courtesy U.S. Army.

the United States to achieve a nuclear test ban treaty. As a result, the Partial Test Ban Treaty of 1963 went into effect and "began Soviet–American détente. The speech was partially written by Norman Cousins, founder and co-chair of the National Committee for a Sane Nuclear Policy, America's largest peace group. Cousins also brokered the treaty."[6]

TEEN ACTIVISM

While numerous organizations currently work for peace, individual young adults are making their mark also. Some teenagers have taken part in PeaceJam, an international organization that encourages youth to be peacemakers in their own communities and the wider world. They are inspired by Nobel peace laureates who personally work with youth to pass on the skills, spirit, and wisdom the Nobel winners exemplify. Other teens attend peace vigils or organize antiwar demonstrations and protests.

Consider teenager Ava Lowery of Alabama. She held her sixteenth birthday party on the steps of the state capitol—actually it was set up as a rally against the Iraq War. She has

PEACE ORGANIZATIONS

Dozens of national organizations promote peace as well as social justice, human rights, and other causes. The following list is just a sampling, and among them are youth groups or organizations that welcome young adults and encourage activism. The descriptions of the organizations come from their websites:

- **American Friends Service Committee** carries out service, development, social justice, and peace programs throughout the world.[7]
- **Baptist Peace Fellowship of North America** gathers, equips, and mobilizes Baptists to build a culture of peace rooted in justice.[8]
- **Campus Antiwar Network** is an independent network of students opposing the occupation of Iraq and military recruiters in schools at campuses all over the country.[9]
- **Central Committee for Conscientious Objectors** supports and promotes individual and collective resistance to war and preparations for war.[10]
- **CODEPINK** is a women-initiated grassroots peace and social justice movement working to end the war in Iraq, stop new wars, and redirect our resources into health care, education, and other life-affirming activities.[11]
- **Fellowship of Reconciliation** is an interfaith organization that seeks to replace violence, war, racism, and economic injustice with nonviolence, peace, and justice.[12]
- **Jeannette Rankin Peace Center** connects and empowers people to build a socially just, nonviolent, and sustainable community and world.[13]
- **Jewish Peace Fellowship** defends the rights of COs and fights for peace and justice.[14]
- **PeaceJam Foundation** is designed to create a new generation of young leaders committed to positive change in themselves, their communities, and the world through the inspiration of Nobel peace laureates.[15]
- **Teens of Peace** is an organization for students in grades 9–12 that encourages spiritual growth among Peace Lutheran members of high school age as well as their friends.[16]

developed a website called PeaceTakesCourage.com and made dozens of animations with soundtracks that include music and comments. She explains, "the media are not showing the real images of the war, so I did a lot [of] research and started my own website."[17]

Lowery's animations often are slideshows of wounded soldiers, mourning Iraqi civilians, and injured and dead children. One especially potent short is called "What Would Jesus Do?" It features a child singing "Jesus loves me, this I know" as photographs show wounded Iraqi children. The video makes the point that Jesus does not differentiate between who is and is not worthy of love. It ends with words from the Beatitudes: "Blessed are they who mourn and Blessed are the meek and Blessed are the merciful and Blessed are the peacemakers."[18] The site has been featured on numerous news shows, in newspaper and magazine articles, and on Internet blogs. While Lowery receives much support, she also gets hate mail with profane language, sexually explicit threats, and accusations of being a traitor and terrorist.

Joseph Murray of Vista, California, is another teenage peace activist. He is a member of the Student Peace Alliance and organized a 2007 march to commemorate the Season for Nonviolence, a two-month "national educational, media, and grassroots campaign dedicated to demonstrating that nonviolence is a powerful way to heal, transform, and empower our lives and our communities," according to the project's website.[19] Murray also attended a National Peace Alliance convention held in Washington, DC, in 2007 and with other delegates lobbied legislators, urging them to establish a U.S. Department of Peace and Nonviolence. Murray told a reporter, "It was incredible, all the support that I saw for this bill. . . . I come from a peace-oriented, extroverted family, but to hear 700 other people speaking the same language was really, really cool."[20]

Teenager Maggie Astor of New Jersey began her antiwar efforts in January 2003 with a petition she circulated in her school to stop the war on Iraq. She explains, "I naively believed my little petition would stop the war," but the invasion began two months later.[21] She was disappointed and angry and thought there was no more she could do. But she discovered the "New Jersey Peace Action (NJPA), an antiwar organization based in Bloomfield, New Jersey. I started volunteering there in January 2005 to fulfill my school's community service requirement. I figured I would do my 30 hours and leave, but somehow 30 hours turned to 50 and then to 100, and the idea of leaving never occurred to me again."[22]

Astor has taken part in peace conferences and met other teen peace activists. She describes the experience as "incredible to meet people my age who thought the same way I did—quite a change from the political apathy of many of my classmates."[23] She has joined efforts to ensure that students and their families can prevent the release of student information to the military. She started a postcard campaign asking the governor to

This *V* for victory and peace sign was first used in Europe during World War II as a symbol of freedom from occupying forces. Since the 1960s, peace movements have used the sign as a symbol of victory for peace and truth. Photo by the author.

THE PEACE CRANE STORY

The atom bomb that the United States dropped on Hiroshima, Japan, not only killed thousands but also had aftereffects, causing cancer and other illnesses among survivors. Young Sadako Sasaki was one who became ill and developed leukemia. While she was hospitalized, one of her friends brought her a folded paper crane. A Japanese legend says that the "crane lives for a thousand years, and a sick person who folds a thousand cranes will become well again," according to Peace Craft, a company inspired by the tradition and committed to helping children.[24] The company's website

An origami peace crane hanging in the author's home. Photo by the author.

explains, "Sadako folded cranes throughout her illness. The flock hung above her bed on strings."[25] She folded 644 cranes before she died, and "classmates folded the remaining . . . cranes, so that one thousand were buried with Sadako."[26] Since then, the origami paper crane has become a symbol that represents a prayer for peace.

pressure the state board of education to establish a statewide policy to send opt-out forms to every student.

Does the peace activism of teenagers as well as that of organized peace groups make a difference in American attitudes toward war? Professor Wittner declares that "additional research on peace movement efficacy" needs to be done, but he adds, "I think it is fair to say that, on numerous occasions, peace activism has exercised a restraining influence on U.S. foreign and military policy."[27] Whether this holds true in current times or in the future is an open question. Nevertheless, countless peace activists will continue their efforts because they firmly believe such a cause will never become outmoded.

NOTES

1. Quoted in Paul Rogat Loeb, "Reclaiming Hope: The Peace Movement after the War," n.d., www.paulloeb.org/articles/reclaiminghope.htm (accessed June 23, 2007).

2. Sue Davidson, *A Heart in Politics: Jeannette Rankin and Patsy T. Mink* (Seattle, WA: Seal Press, 1994), pp. 45–46.

3. President John F. Kennedy, 1963 Commencement Speech, American University, June 10, 1963, www.american.edu/media/speeches/Kennedy.htm (accessed June 23, 2007).

4. Lawrence S. Wittner, "Have Peace Activists Ever Stopped a War?" n.d., www.lewrockwell.com/wittner/wittner17.html (accessed June 23, 2007).

5. Wittner, "Have Peace Activists Ever Stopped a War?"

6. Wittner, "Have Peace Activists Ever Stopped a War?"

7. See www.afsc.org/about/default.htm (accessed June 23, 2007).

8. See www.bpfna.org/about (accessed June 23, 2007).

9. See www.campusantiwar.net/index.php?option=content&task=view&id=93&Itemid=52 (accessed June 23, 2007).

10. See www.objector.org/ccco/whoweare.html (accessed June 23, 2007).

11. See www.codepinkalert.org/article.php?list=type&type=3 (accessed June 23, 2007).

12. See www.forusa.org/about/vismis.html (accessed June 23, 2007).

13. See www.jrpc.org (accessed June 23, 2007).

14. See www.jewishpeacefellowship.org (accessed June 23, 2007).

15. See www.peacejam.org/about.htm (accessed June 23, 2007).

16. See www.peacehartford.org/site/default.asp?sec_id=2830 (accessed June 23, 2007).

17. Quoted in Matthew Rothschild, "Animation Producer Gets Ugly Slurs," *The Progressive*, April 24, 2006, progressive.org/mag_mc042406 (accessed June 26, 2007).

18. See Matthew 5:3–12 in the King James version of the Bible.

19. Association for Global New Thought, "2007 Gandhi and King: A Season for Nonviolence," n.d., www.agnt.org/snv02.htm (accessed June 26, 2007).

20. Quoted in Shayna Chabner, "Vista Teen Takes to Heart Message of Peace, Nonviolence," *North County Times*, February 2, 2007, nctimes.com/articles/2007/02/19/news/top_stories/21807190822.prt (accessed June 23, 2007).

21. Maggie Astor, "Peace Activism: From the Mundane to the Memorable," *Teen Voices.com*, December 2006, www.teenvoices .com/issue_current/tvteen_activist_december06.html (accessed June 23, 2007).

22. Astor, "Peace Activism."

23. Astor, "Peace Activism."

24. Peace Craft, "Story of Sadako," n.d., www.peacecraft.cc/story_of_sadako.html (accessed June 26, 2007).

25. Peace Craft, "Story of Sadako."

26. Peace Craft, "Story of Sadako."

27. Wittner, "Have Peace Activists Ever Stopped a War?"

Resources

BOOKS

Appy, Christian G. *Patriots: The Vietnam War Remembered from All Sides*. New York: Penguin Books, 2003.

Dann, John C., ed. *The Revolution Remembered: Eyewitness Accounts of the War for Independence*. Chicago: University of Chicago Press, 1980.

Falk, Candace Serena. *Love, Anarchy, and Emma Goldman*. New York: Holt, Rinehart and Winston, 1984; reprint, New Brunswick, NJ: Rutgers University Press, 1990.

Gay, Kathlyn, and Christine Whittington. *Body Marks: Tattooing, Piercing, and Scarification*. Brookfield, CT: Twenty-First Century Books, 2002.

Greene, Bob. *Homecoming: When the Soldiers Returned from Vietnam*. New York: G. P. Putnam's Sons, 1989.

Holm, Tom. *Strong Hearts, Wounded Souls: Native American Veterans of the Vietnam War*. Austin: University of Texas Press, 1996.

Latty, Yvonne. *We Were There: Voices of African American Veterans, from World War II to the War in Iraq*. With photographs by Ron Tarver. New York: Amistad/HarperCollins, 2004.

Laufer, Peter. *Mission Rejected: U.S. Soldiers Who Say No to Iraq*. Foreword by Norman Solomon. White River Junction, VT: Chelsea Green, 2006.

Leahy, J. F. *Honor, Courage, Commitment: Navy Boot Camp*. Annapolis: Naval Institute Press, 2002.

Zinn, Howard. *A People's History of the United States: 1492–Present*. New York: HarperCollins, 2003.

MAGAZINE ARTICLES

"Voices of the Fallen.," *Newsweek*, Special Issue, April 2, 2007.

Mariscal, Jorge. "The Poverty Draft: Do Military Recruiters Disproportionately Target Communities of Color and the Poor?" *Sojourners Magazine*, June 2007. Available online at www.sojo.net/index.cfm?action=magazine.article& issue=soj0706&article=070628 (accessed January 4, 2008).

Meacham, Jon. "Our Soldiers' Stories: The War in the Words of the Dead." Editorial. *Newsweek*, Special Issue, April 2, 2007, p. 24.

Phillips, Rebecca. "Beliefwatch: Foxholes." *Newsweek*, August 21, 2006. Available online at www.newsweek.com/id/46411 (accessed January 21, 2008).

WEBSITES

Association of the U.S. Army. www.ausa.org.

Documenting the American South. docsouth.unc.edu/support/about.

Independence Hall Association. 12.164.81.10/paine/index.htm.

Military Working Dog Foundation. www.militaryworkingdog.com/history.

Teen Ink. teenink.com.

U.S. Air Force. www.airforce.com.

U.S. Air Force Academy. www.usafa.af.mil.

U.S. Coast Guard Academy. www.cga.edu.

U.S. Department of Defense. www.defenselink.mil.

U.S. Merchant Marine Academy. www.usmma.edu.

U.S. Military Academy. www.usma.edu.

U.S. Naval Academy. www.nadn.navy.mil.

U.S. Navy. www.navy.com.

Index

About the Author

Kathlyn Gay is the author of more than 120 books on diverse topics. Scarecrow Press has published four of her titles: *Religion and Spirituality: The Ultimate Teen Guide* (2006), *Volunteering: The Ultimate Teen Guide* (2004), *Cultural Diversity: Conflicts and Challenges: The Ultimate Teen Guide* (2003), and *Epilepsy: The Ultimate Teen Guide* (2002).